ISLAM
AND TEMPORAL POWER

Bojan Petrović

Kendall Hunt
publishing company

Cover images courtesy author
Cover provided by Vesna Petrović

Kendall Hunt
publishing company

www.kendallhunt.com
Send all inquiries to:
4050 Westmark Drive
Dubuque, IA 52004-1840

Printed in the United States of America
10 9 8 7 6 5 4 3

For my mother
Belka

CONTENTS

ACKNOWLEDGMENT

Many people have been supportive in the production of this book. At Kendall Hunt the most important are Jason McFaul and Linda Chapman. I have been fortunate to have a very talented assistant Amir Fatollahi who provided research support on two of the book chapters and raised several critical questions. I owe much to my students at University of California at Irvine and at University of California at Los Angeles for their persistent questioning during my lectures, which deepened my understanding and clarified my own thinking about the issues discussed in the book. A special thanks goes to Vesna Petrović, my tireless supporter, who read and criticized earlier drafts of this book and designed the book covers.

INTRODUCTION

A few weeks into 2011, successive public protests led to the fall of three Arab political regimes: first in Tunisia, soon after in Egypt, and months later in Libya. Some protesters reacted to the decades of police brutality and political repression, others to the government's economic policies that induced inequality and polarized society. The end of the three authoritarian regimes marked the first-ever successful bottom-up challenge to political rule in the Middle East and North Africa (MENA) and encouraged protesters elsewhere in the region to persist in challenging their unaccountable political rulers. Anti-government protests rapidly spread to most of the MENA states, encompassing Algeria, Jordan, Yemen, Bahrain, Saudi Arabia, and Syria. In Egypt and Tunisia, the military, the strongest national institution in both, moved to fill in the ensuing power vacuum, while civilian transitional government has done so in Libya. Whether political pluralism will follow and become institutionalized in a democratic form in any of the three, or any of the additional MENA cases, is difficult to anticipate and may remain undetermined for years to come. Nevertheless, the political space in Tunisia and Egypt has already changed in the sense that actors best organized and positioned to take advantage of the end of the old regime have asserted their role in the first general elections. As in the earlier electoral outcomes in the majority-Arab states between 1989 and 2011—Jordan (1989), Algeria (1991), Egypt (2005), Iraq (2005), and Palestinian territories (2006)—the political groups that emerged as prominent are the so-called Islamist organizations.

Who are Islamists? What are their objectives? What explains the spread of their ideas? How have they emerged as the actors best organized to compete in elections? Islamists are Muslims who believe that Islamic theology and jurisprudence should become an authoritative frame of reference in the public sphere.[1] They are engaged in a variety of national and transnational movements, party organizations, and activist groups whose aim is to strengthen Islamic influences in political, economic, and social life.[2] Some are driven to Islamism by their holistic view of religion, one that holds that God has revealed a law governing the whole of human affairs. They endorse an organic vision of ordering society, political life, and education in terms of Islamic principles and go so far as to deny secular justification of political rule altogether. Others adopt Islamism as a way of coping with a spiritual vacuum resulting from modern day materialism and ubiquitous rationality devoid of divinity. Similar to traditional, more conservative segments of society in the West, these groups oppose moral guidance dictated by personal, utilitarian calculations and the turning of the self-interest behavior into a universal human attribute. For yet others, removed from longstanding local identities by the processes of economic modernization and social change throughout the world, a process often described as globalization, Islamism is a way of creating identity. For young, college-educated, middle-class technicians, professionals, and business persons, Islam fills this gap. This is similar to movements in Western Christianity, Judaism, Buddhism, and Hinduism, which are often labeled "fundamentalist."

Many Muslims view Western policies since the nineteenth century as having helped block the freedoms necessary to develop their personal and national capacities in ways comparable to developed countries; they regard the international order as skewed against them and their interests. Islamists often seek to channel this general Muslim grievance by asserting the primacy of their religious identity as an important tool of mobilizing for political and military purposes. Throughout the history of Islamic civilization, re-assertion of religious piety and society-wide transformation helped restore political unity and group solidarity in the Muslim community. Historically, Islam served as the force for mobilizing masses against external, non-Muslim influence in the early centuries of Islamic civilization (e.g., Persian, Byzantine, and Mongol) or the nineteenth and twentieth century colonial rule (against the French, British, Italian, and the Dutch, for example). The tradition of political resistance in the name of religious purity spans from the succession of Prophet Muhammad in the seventh century AD to the attempts of Sharrif Hussayn, the governor of the city of Mecca, to challenge what he perceived as atheistic governance of the Young Turks in the last decades of the Ottoman Empire in the early twentieth century. Contemporary Islamism provided a means for political mobilization and opposition to incumbent political regimes (e.g, Jordan and Algeria) and provided a driving force for mobilizing against the perceived oppression of Muslim population (e.g., Chechnya, Kashmir, Bosnia and Herzegovina, Mindanao, and Palestinian territories).

Some of the most influential views of contemporary Islamists date back to the rise of so-called Islamist nationalism in South Asia and the creation of an organization of Muslim Brothers in the Middle East (Egypt, Jordan, Syria, and Palestinian territories) in the early decades of the twentieth century, when the idea of society-wide transformation of Muslim societies guided by religion once again gained currency. Looking back at the structures of the classical Islamic state, Islamists saw the connection between religious piety of rulers and good and just governance. By reasserting the role of religion in the public sphere, they sought to restore what they perceived as the state's lost political legitimacy. Initially some have attempted to do so through grass-roots activism, i.e., through the bottom up Islamization of society, most prominently by the founder of Muslim Brothers, Hasan al Banna in Egypt. Others, like Sayyid Abul A'la Al-Mawdudi, Sayeed Qutb, and Ruhollah Khomeini—each within their respective national contexts of Pakistan, Egypt, and Iran—did not see much potential for change in a bottom up Islamization in the presence of the secular state and its formidable powers over society. Taking cues from the Leninist strategy of revolutionary political change, they instead adopted the strategy of conquering the modern state as necessary in order to conduct a top-down societal transformation in the spirit of Islamic values and principles. These Islamists envisioned "government run by them, according to the *sharia* law and Islamic values as they define and apply them."[3] Initially, the relative strength of secularist nationalist ideas limited the influence that Islamism exerted on the Muslims outside of the Middle East and South Asia. But by the 1960s, a set of domestic and international developments spurred religious consciousness throughout much of the Muslim world.[4]

Domestically, the authoritarian nature of most of the majority-Muslim incumbent regimes (e.g., Iran, Turkey, Algeria, Afghanistan, and Egypt) generated dissatisfaction and provoked political opposition from a variety of ideological points of view. Although liberal political groups in some national contexts played an important role in challenging the incumbent regimes (e.g., Iran, Egypt, and Lebanon), Marxist-Leninist and Islamist movements and organizations often played a more prominent role. In the 1970s, (secular) governments of Egypt, Jordan, Pakistan, Malaysia, Indonesia, and Sudan found it politically opportunistic to support various Muslim movements at home in order to marginalize forces of the political left (Marxist groups).[5] Gradual marginalization of the political left in a number of Muslim countries, in the course of and following the Cold War, combined with relatively weak liberal groups in the individual national contexts, often left Islamists as the only viable political force in the position to challenge the incumbent authoritarian regimes. Islamists' political calls for justice by doing away with corruption and foreign influence had an enormous appeal (e.g., Iran). Their religious credentials often appealed to the devout masses, while their active efforts at providing social services in the absence of state policies and state inefficiencies (e.g., Egypt and Lebanon) further bolstered their legitimacy. At the international level, the fall of Jerusalem to the Israeli forces after the 1967 war, the success of Iranian revolution in January of 1979, and the Soviet invasion of Afghanistan later that same year successively provided the catalyst for the diffusion of Islamist ideas across the world. Moreover, as some Islamists began building transnational ties, the idealized myth of the Islamic community (umma) started to take shape.

Islamist organizations and movements from Morocco to the Philippines share the view of the need to restore the role of religion in the public sphere by applying Islamic law. While the sharia is grounded in the absolute and its authority does not depend on any specific temporal state, there is no agreement as to what constitutes it besides the Quran. Moreover, it is not at all clear what exactly it means nowadays to apply Islamic law—including some of its harshest sanctions—in the Muslim-populated states where there is much ideological variation ranging from ultra-conservativism (e.g., Saudi Arabia) to selective political liberalism (e.g., Turkey and Mali). As a result, among the Muslims worldwide, the debate is going on over the substance and scope of the implementation of the sharia. Is religion the best means (method) to create social order? Is social order more important than political order? Seemingly more numerous, Islamist modernists perceive liberal ideals of justice and reason as the core of Islamic truth and argue that Islam is entirely compatible with modern life.[6] They call for the restoration of common rituals such as prayers or charitable giving, but also claim to value democratic participation and be in favor of political rights. For example, Egypt's Muslim Brotherhood and Tunisia's al-Nahda party claim that they would not universally impose sharia law and that they would uphold women's rights, refrain from forcing women to wear the veil, and respect ethnic and religious minorities.

In contrast, the less numerous ultra-conservative *Salafists* (literalists and purists as they are also called) believe in a theocratic Muslim state or, in the European context, such as in the United Kingdom and the Netherlands, seek the creations of pure Islamic enclaves that would be attentive to the formalistic and public rituals of Islam that impose draconian laws. They call for the rejection of civil institutions, refuse to participate in the political process, enforce social uniformity, and re-instate punishment for vices (e.g, adultery, alcohol drinking, etc.). On the extreme end in this camp are those who call for the restoration of Islam's medieval rules of war and political domination and who openly advocate the use of violence (a call for offensive *jihad*). Although they all claim to share the strategic goal of creating an Islamic state, there is a variation among them: some are aiming to do so within the national borders (implicitly accepting the system of nation-states), others as a regional caliphate (the political entity uniting the Muslim community in early Islam), and yet others are talking about the restoration of the old caliphate that in early Islam encompassed areas between western Africa and south Asia (in a clear denial of the system of nation-states).

In practice, the outlined differences in objectives between the two groups are not so neatly divided. They are sometimes more obvious (as in Egypt, Indonesia, and Pakistan) but at other times may be deliberately less so (as in the case of Hezbollah in Lebanon or Hamas in Palestinian territories). Among the Muslims worldwide, it is not uncommon to sympathize with a cause (or some of the causes) of a group but not necessarily agree with all its actions, its organization, or its (often militant) ideology/worldview. For the outsiders, on the other hand, there are common misperceptions of individual Islamic groups; some mistake extremists for moderates and equate calls for Islamization in individual national contexts with a totalitarian movement. At the same time, even those organizations and movements that are committed to working within democratic institutions sometimes promote values at odds with progressive standards of freedom, equality, and tolerance.

Islamism varies in intensity and strategic and tactical objectives both across nations and time. But is it here to stay or is just an episode in a broader historical perspective? This book aims to answer this question by looking at Islamic political tradition and the historical shifts in the relationship between Islam and the temporal powers of the Muslim state. It discusses this relationship specifically in three distinct historical epochs: the first is the period following the rapid expansion of the early

Islamic community between the seventh and tenth centuries AD; the second traces the effects of the system of nation states on Muslims worldwide between the last decade of the nineteenth century and the early 1960s; and the third starts with the quest for accountable governance in the Muslim state in the 1970s and continues to the present. This book demonstrates how Islamism took shape a few decades into the second historical epoch of the creation of nation states, thus partially overlapping with it, and then intensified in the third epoch, that of the quest of accountable governance in the state. The three-part structure of this book directly reflects this analytical framework.

This review of history is aimed at substantiating the central claim of the book that Islamism is a historical phenomenon, a response to the set of social, economic, and political conditions, rather than an inevitable consequence of the firmly fixed relationship between Islam and temporal power in a Muslim state. It offers a partial historical account of the state formation in parts of the Muslim world necessary to highlight the major shifts in that process. Geographically, it focuses on the core Muslim Middle Eastern countries in terms of their population size and/or their political relevance (Egypt, Iran, Turkey, and Saudi Arabia) and makes occasional references to Muslim countries in Western Africa (Morocco), South and Southeast Asia (Pakistan and Indonesia respectively) among others. The book further identifies some of the key variables important in comparing and contrasting various Islamist organizations and movements especially with respect to the issue of whether their Islamism is driven by domestic politics or by external factors. Finally, while it offers a nuanced account of the relationship between Islam and politics it seeks to stay clear of theological disputes within Islam.

Finally, a few words that I believe help underline the relevance of this book: The constitutional place of Islam is one of the most significant political issues in both Muslim-majority and Muslim-minority states and in large part defines the relationship between the two. One in four of the world's population is Muslim. Although territorially based initially on the Arabian Peninsula, Islamic civilization spread both eastward and westward. As a result, now nearly two out of three of the world's Muslims live in Asia while the number of Muslims in India, where Hindus constitute a majority, exceeds the number of Muslims in any other country except in Indonesia and Pakistan, and more than twice as many as in Egypt. Similarly, the large concentration of Muslims in Russia, China, Germany, and France questions the validity of a category of a non-Muslim state in opposition to a Muslim one. It also points out that the role of Islam in a state could not be isolated as a question in a single national context but is rather of global relevance. Islamism, on the other hand, is a source of conflict, sometimes violent, not just with non-Muslims but also among Muslims themselves. Understanding Islam's historical origins could provide a clue to Islamism's possible withering away.

PART ONE

From a City-State to a Caliphate

CHAPTER 1

Faith, Communal Solidarity, and Political Authority

According to Islam, the implementation of God's will, as the defining feature of being Muslim, is not simply an individual act.[1] It requires the creation of a just social order that operates by Islamic precepts.[2] Aside from custom and tradition, it is Muslims' religious beliefs that are deemed necessary to guide their actions and provide order and regularity in their community. Since their social conduct is regulated (and reinforced) by their religious beliefs, which the Muslim community holds in common by virtue of sharing the faith, social norms thus established need no justification outside of the religious realm. Knowledge of religious norms of conduct thus has a dual function: it organizes the daily life of practitioners and at the same time facilitates the governance of the religious community (umma) as a whole. In so doing, it creates a unity of moral, political, and religious spheres in the umma. In order to preserve this unique and tacitly agreed upon social ground, the strength of the ties of the spiritual community of believers plays a paramount role.[3] This is why solidarity ('asabīyah) under God and His Prophet became a political imperative for the umma and provided the key objective of political authority. The Muslim faith in God, as both the symbol of strength of the umma and the primary source of communal solidarity, thus secured unity of thought, provided justification of social norms, and legitimated political authority and action.[4] Hence the appeal to many practicing Muslims of a holistic view of Islam as a religion that encompasses both politics and society.[5]

Political imperatives of the umma made faith and power firmly intertwined.[6] The Quran taught that a society which lived according to God's will could not fail. Divine guidance helped Prophet Mohammad (570–632) secure social unity, while his personal political success in sustaining it endorsed the Muslim faith in God. The Prophet's arbitration skills in resolving disputes earned him the title "al Amin," the trusted one. His ability to manage social and political discord also helped him firmly establish his political authority.[7] In the course of his governance in what would develop initially into the city-state of Medina, Muhammad's implementation of social justice, racial equality, and a fair distribution of wealth not only solidified the Muslim faith in God but also provided legitimacy to his rule. The Muslims constituted a new community of believers, led by the Prophet's practical and spiritual guidance, and created a model for others to emulate. Community was to a large extent personal and familiar, composed of cohesive and relatively homogenous people, uniting them in their beliefs. In this community (relatively small by the standards of the average-sized modern-day nation-state, let alone of successive multiple-continents-wide empires that the *umma* subsequently grew into), the political power, if intertwined with faith, did not establish primacy over religious sphere.

What was the purpose of political power in early Islam? It was similar to the purpose of political power in any other community: to maintain social unity and reach decisions binding on all members of the community. But it was applied to a community with a high level of collective decency secured by the common faith.[8] The divinely justified governance called on both rulers and ruled to be responsible to God with whom sovereignty lies. A governing decision (via this divine mandate) seldom required enforcement, while its legitimacy stemmed from the ruler's piousness, his character, and his moral virtues rather than simply from the rational notion of efficacy of his rule. Nevertheless, in the early days of Islam, the issue of mutual obligations between rulers and ruled was a subject of debate.[9]

Islam solidified a new universalist moral order, which stressed a common religious faith (in God's will) and downplayed tribal ties that structured social relations on the Arabian peninsula prior to the initiation of Islam in the seventh century AD.[10] This new normative system, based on Quranic principles that among other things promoted equity, mercy, justice, and perhaps most prominently the right of women to own property, distinguished itself from the Bedouine customs and culture that preceded it. It called for actions that were to be judged by their moral intentions and the implementation of norms by moral example rather than by compulsion and the use of force.[11] The Prophet, as a principle source of moral example, sought not to separate himself in dress or manner from the community he came to rule. He was tightly integrated with the Islamic community to whom this emerging normative system was binding. This emphasis on emulation and correct ritualistic practice (or orthopraxy) was a true proof of the faith. But it was not necessarily meant to establish uniformity of social life.

Islam could thus be realized only by the creation of a religiously guided community. A unifying political leadership facilitated the creation of a new political organization that was entirely centered on the Prophet. Since Muhammad was the last in the line of the prophets to be exposed to God's revelations, no improvements on the rightly guided life of the Prophet's community should have followed.[12] Abandoning the Prophet's model of community amounted to renouncing God and to slipping back into the pre-Islamic state of ignorance of divine guidance (*jahiliyya*) while engaging in innovation (*bida*) that would bypass any of the essential principles revealed to Muhammad, and practiced by him during his lifetime, would lead to the abandonment of faith, i.e., apostasy. The features of the early Islamic polity would have lasting impact on a number of politically relevant issues such as leadership, succession, legitimacy, and primary communal identity.

CHAPTER 2

Sources of Plurality in Early Islam

Although initiated in the Bedouine Arabian culture, Islamic doctrine is universalist; it is intended not as a religion of a specific tribe, ethnic group, or nation, nor as a faith limited to specific geographic territory. Islam is a religion to which any people anywhere in the world may convert.[1] It contains absolute moral truths applicable to all people at all times. According to God's will declared in the *Quran*, the newly constituted Muslim community of believers built on a moral social order was to become an example to other communities.[2] But who would act as a leader of this community after Muhammad's passing in 632 AD? Could the community's original model of divine governance be preserved with the diffusion of Islam? How was civil order in the community to be preserved in the absence of divinely mandated legitimacy? Was there a need for the development of new institutions? What will be the nature of the Muslim community's encounters and exchanges with other, non-Bedouine cultures? Is Islam primarily oriented toward the inward side of the human existence or is it mostly oriented towards its outward manifestations?

The *umma* that Muhammad left behind after his death was entirely centered on him. His access to divine revelations, combined with his military and leadership skills, established him as a political and religious authority in the *umma*. After his death, no single human being could possibly combine all of his roles and execute moral powers that he had accumulated in his lifetime. The Prophet's death triggered political struggles of succession over religious authority and the right to governance in the community and led eventually to a sectarian split. The continuing expansion of the Muslim community between the eighth and the tenth centuries AD challenged its original mode of governance as it gradually developed into state structures resembling those of the Byzantine and Persian empires of the time. Islam's encounters with diverse cultural traditions into which it expanded, the growing size and the changing demographic structure of its community, sometimes collided with the Bedouine culture in which the religion originated. While for some Muslims Islam manifested an inward, mystical side, others stressed outward set of codes and institutions.[3] In sum, although the faith in one God and the Prophet as his messenger persisted, some of the community's practices in the *umma* inevitably changed with the growth in its size and the passage of time. However, the question of how far everyday practices may depart from those of the Prophet's community without subverting Islam would remain an open one.

Struggles over Succession

The role of the *umma*'s political-religious leader passed to a series of caliphs (Arabic for "substitute"). But the differences over the selection criteria for caliphs— blood relationship to the Prophet, familiarity with his practices, personal piety, divinely mandated legitimacy, and ability to discern God's will—produced factions and initiated struggles of succession within the community. Mohammad's immediate successor was to be chosen between his descendent cousin and son-in-law 'Ali bin Abu Talib and Abu Bakr, the prophet's companion and leader believed to be the most likely to follow closely the tenets of the faith. Although the support for the latter prevailed, and the first three of the Prophet's successors came from the group of his companions, the issue of succession did not get resolved. 'Ali's supporters assassinated Caliph Uthman, the third of the so-called "rightly guided" caliphs, while 'Ali's right to the caliphate itself was soon contested by Mu'awiyah, the governor from a wealthy and powerful clan of the Umayyads (who opposed Muhammad during his lifetime).[4]

The first civil war that followed pitted the followers of 'Ali (Shi'a 'Ali) against the Umayyads and produced yet another Islamic faction, the Kharjites, who took it upon themselves to carry the banner for Islamic purity. Taking personal piety to be the sole measure of a person's right to lead, the Kharijities eventually turned against 'Ali himself and assassinated him in 661 AD. Moreover, by extending the test of personal piety to the members of the entire community, they massacred scores of Muslims in Arabia claiming that they were infidels.[5] By ending 'Ali's caliphate, the Kharjites made the question of who determines what is right and wrong at the highest level the prominent one. Their claim was that "the imam" (another term for a successor) is not one with the extraordinary ability to discern God's will, as 'Ali's supporters claimed. Rather, it was supposed to be the most deserving person in the community.

'Ali's death was a turning point for early Islam as the list of the Prophet's close personal followers had been exhausted.[6] The issue of whether civil order within the *umma* is more important than the divinely mandated legitimacy of its leadership came to the forefront. 'Ali's challenger Mu'awiyah was soon recognized as caliph throughout the empire and became the founder of the Umayyad dynasty (661–750). He was a pragmatic ruler whose principal concerns were continued expansion of Islamic territories, management of the state's resources, and consolidation of his dynasty.[7] A separate community, refusing to recognize the authority of the Umayyad caliphs recognized only the successors to 'Ali as authorities (what will eventually become *Shiism* after Shi'ati 'Ali or 'Ali's supporters) and gave these successors the title "imam." The martyrdom of 'Ali, and later that of his son Hussein who unsuccessfully challenged Mu'awiyah's rule, as the founding imams, profoundly shaped the politics and theology of *Shiism*. It led to the largest division within the Muslim community—that between the *Shi'ati* and the *Sunni*—without any drastic variation in fundamental beliefs or practices.

Throughout the Umayyad rule, the religious idealists took on the function of a moralistic oppositional force.[8] Like the followers of 'Ali and the Kharjites, discussed above, the 'Abassids too believed that the spirit of Islam had been betrayed by what they perceived as secular-minded Umayyads. As Muhammad's relatives, the 'Abassids' pietism had a concrete character to it. They accused the government for being impious, for making "innovations" of Islamic practices instead of following the way of the Prophet, and claimed that it had forgotten its communal obligations in favor of material advantages for the few.[9] In 740 AD, fearing internal disintegration of the community, a coalition of interest groups and sects, including the Shia (who still bore a grudge against the Umayyads) launched another civil war that ended the establishment of the Umayyad dynasty in 750 AD. Nevertheless, religious purity—the need of true Islamic guidance for the community—continued to play a role in determining legitimacy of the rule in early Islam.[10] The idea of establishing a new and improved alternative society, one that is genuinely Islamic and nothing like the societies that already existed, and which ought to be modeled after the Prophet's city-state in Medina, would live on. Other ideas will be discussed in a later section.

Arab Beduine Heritage and Cultural Exchange

As discussed above, the religious beliefs of the Muslim community's members guided their actions and provided order and regularity. So, to an extent, did their Arab Bedouin customs and traditions, independent of formal theology. In that sense, early Islam favored customs of the region of its origin.[11] It facilitated the spread of Arabic into other regions—Persian, Semitic, North African, Hellenistic—as both "the daily language and the holy language."[12] For example, the Umayyads (Al-Walid 705–715 AD), having conquered Egypt changed it from "a Coptic speaking Christian society into an Arabic speaking one" and instituted Arabic as the only official language of the empire (in all administration). The diffusion of Arabic, the spread of its linguistic, religious, and social influences, cemented the primacy of the Bedouine culture in much of the Islamic world where the Arabic script, if not the language itself, connotes Muslim identity to this day. This is why Islam, in its early development, was perceived externally as an exclusively Arab religion often discriminating against non-Arab converts.[13] The Umayyad ruling elite for the most part, save the exceptions discussed below, discriminated against non-Arabs but the 'Abassid caliphate (758–1258 AD) relationship to non-Arabs was more complex. The Abbasids (750–1258 CE) adopted a universalist policy of accepting the equality of all Muslims, regardless of their ethnic origins.[14] Militarily, it relied heavily on so-called client (*mawali*) Muslims (foreigners who had converted to Islam); however, it still treated them as foreigners who could not be incorporated into the kinship-based Arab society. The *mawali* had to be voluntarily included into the protection of a clan and thus become the clan's "clients," which still made them, for the most part, the second-class citizens despite being Muslims nominally.

However, the primacy of Bedouin culture was difficult to sustain in the expanding empire. As the number of non-Arab Muslim converts increased, the primacy of

Arabs and their Bedouine culture became challenged. One prominent example is that of the Islamic culture that grew on the Spanish soil, the Moorish culture, which was dramatically different from the Iranian-Semitic culture that grew up around the 'Abbasid caliphate. Over time, the large numbers of Berber-speaking and Persian-speaking Muslims threatened the primacy of the very language upon which Islam was based. But it was not just the language that was challenged. Nomadic and sedentary Arabs were accustomed to the tribal patriarchal model followed by the early caliphs. With the onset of the Arab conquests and the differentiation of state institutions (already under the second caliph Umar), the governance no longer benefited from reinforcing tribal, ethnic, and other solidarities.[15] Political concepts derived from the nomadic tribe (e.g., the concept of consultation) proved unsuitable to a large, partly urbanized state, as well as to the growing empire.

Durable political arrangements have often been made possible due to the introduction of new concepts derived from regions, which have been conquered.[16] For example, in the early process of expansion, Umar allowed subject populations to retain their religion, language, customs, and government relatively untouched. The Umayyads allowed administrative practices and local customs in conquered territories to be sustained in order to extract a special poll tax (jizyah) as a revenue source.[17] They moved the political center from Mecca on the Arabian Peninsula to Damascus, which prompted some factions to oppose the favoring of Syrians over other Arabs and the centralized control over the distribution of revenues. Their imperial rule was deemed by many to be incompatible with traditional Arab values.[18]

The Abbasids, on their part, had adopted the Byzantine model of administration—specifically by introducing taxation and bringing the military under the financial control of the state—and employed significant numbers of non-Arabs. The Abbasids centralized political authority, turning a caliph into an absolutist monarch who exercised the powers of both secular king and spiritual head of the Islamic umma.[19] By moving the Islamic political center from Damascus (Syria) to Baghdad (Iraq), they brought Islam into close contact with Iranian (Sasanid) imperial traditions (e.g., royal absolutism and bureaucratic specialization). Abbasid administration was thus modeled on Sasanian imperial administration and employed large numbers of converted Iranians in the increasingly elaborate bureaucratic structure.[20] In so doing they too distanced themselves from their Semitic origins and accelerated the cultural divisions in the world of Islam.

Unity of religious practices, combined with cultural diversity was a constant feature of formative Islam. Secular Greek philosophers and the aristocratic high culture of the royal courts, in addition to the pre-Islamic folk practices, significantly influenced the Islamic dynasties.[21] While Islam created a civilization in the Arabian Peninsula and North Africa, it benefited from the encounters with pre-existing civilizations in the areas it expanded into such as the Maghreb, Andalusia, Persia, the Balkans, and the Javanese and Malay states in Southeast Asia.[22] There it found a rich repository of centuries of accumulated intellectual exchanges and administrative practices. The emerging Islamic civilization was therefore a synthesis of pluralistic cultural and linguistic tendencies; from Arab exceptionalism, it developed into Islamic pluralism or even hybrid identities. In the Moorish markets of tenth-century Andalusia, for example, there were many devout Muslims who could not speak Arabic and Christians who could. Those who remained Christian in belief but Muslim in culture and language were called *Mozarabs* ("almost Arabs") and developed a distinctive culture (architecture, rites). From the Rashidun caliphs to the Abbasids, the emerging class of Islamic scholars made a sustained effort to accommodate the *Quranic* revelations to the traditions of the long-established cultures over which the caliphs came to rule.[23] But this dynamic fusion of cultures seemed to have abandoned the precepts of divine guidance—one recurring theme that prompted later religious movements to restore the conditions of a pious early community.

Efficacy of Political and Military Rule

Prophet Muhammad's immediate followers could build on his achievements by maintaining the spirit of solidarity and piety that brought such triumph to the Prophet. For many Muslims, the first four (pious) caliphs, the patriarchs or patriarchal caliphs of Islam, marked the golden age of Islamic government when a true Islamic polity was in existence. During the era of the Rightly Guided (the Rashidun), the caliphs functioned as first among equals and lived modestly on the model established by Muhammad. Their accountability to the *umma* was based on their political (and military) successes, their religious piety, and the morality of their acts.

Religion legitimated their political action and authority and at the same time presumably tamed power and imposed a morally responsible order on the exercise of power.

However, a unifying political leadership modeled on the Prophet and the pious Rashidun caliphs was difficult to maintain with more complex governance structures. This was especially true with respect to the enforcement of policies and the management of internal social and political discord. As the community continued to expand, despite internal troubles of succession, reconciling the requirements of political efficacy and divine guidance became much more difficult.[24] The epoch of the Arab conquests and the Islamic empire began to develop administrative structure with the second caliph, Umar.[25] Later, during the empire's great expansion under the Umayyads (661–750 AD)—within 100 years of the Prophet's death—Arab forces had reached the Indian subcontinent in the east, and in the west had occupied Spain and crossed the Pyrenees into France.[26]

The expanding governing structures increasingly required greater efficiency in obtaining revenues, more efficient state administration in regulating progressively developing commercial enterprises, and bringing the military under financial control of the state. In sum, the need for greater centralization of the state's powers emerged. The new institutions were developed by the increasingly complex state. An urbanized society—ruled first from Medina then from Damascus—could not easily be administered through the application of a small number of criminal-law rules and principles in the classical Islamic law. The increased number of regulations issued by the ruler led to the differentiation of the administrative entity and the development of administrative law.[27] Islamic law became the primary cohesive force in maintaining social (and political) order. It developed into a comprehensive legal system based on the Quran but not restricted to it. The political system was justified by law and administered through law.

As the frequency of social (and political) discord increased, the solidarity of community became more challenging to maintain despite the unity of faith. The preservation of internal social order increasingly became removed from the ethical sphere of face-to-face interactions of the relatively small original Muslim community and more dependent on the top-down exercise of political power of the emerging empire. As a result, the caliphate came to resemble a "regular" (monarchical state).

Although justified by the theological doctrine, governing actions were increasingly based on utilitarian calculations (rather than on moral intentions). This unification through the influence of political power rather than through the authority derived from divine right eventually created an uneasy relationship between the temporal political power and the pious Muslim community of the caliphate. The Umayyads gradually distanced themselves from the population, took pleasure from the riches that flowed into the treasury, and became less consultative and more authoritarian. They separated their court from the *umma* and surrounded themselves with wealth and ceremony and increasingly appeared as secular leaders whose authority rested primarily on their political power and only marginally on their religious legitimacy. As the Umayyad caliphate introduced a hereditary dynasty in lieu of a succession of rulers sanctioned by a small group of powerful tribal leaders, it seemed that the Muslim community was moving in the direction of alternative justification of political rule. The Umayyad rule gave the appearance of the separation of faith and political power.

The Dispersal of Religious Authority

By virtue of his access to divine guidance, the Prophet could combine the spiritual and political authority in the early Islamic community and thus establish supreme authority over the norms of social conduct in it. After his death, however, no single individual or group was deemed to have inherited all of the powers he accumulated—spiritual, moral, legislative, and executive. The role of the political-spiritual leader passed to a series of caliphs who continued to possess Muhammad's spiritual and legislative authority but at the same time lacked his access to revelation. Though not prophets, they had religious as well as political authority, interpreting as well as enforcing divine decrees. The Prophet's successors found themselves in a difficult position in cases in which complex normative (moral or legal) matters would occur.[28] The *Quran* has a limited number of verses that give legal proscriptions or spell out prohibitions. If it did not speak clearly to a particular question, the first four caliphs (Muhammad's companions) might have been able to make authoritative normative claims based on their proximity to the Prophet himself during his lifetime. But once they were gone, a vacuum in legislative authority followed.

The answer that developed over the first couple of centuries of Islam was that the *Quran* could be supplemented by reference to the prophet's sayings (*hadith*)—quoting Muhammad when he was not in the state of receiving revelations. Prophet Muhammad's actions and words were captured orally, beginning with a person who witnessed the action or statement firsthand. But much of the *hadith* that proliferated over time and across the progressively expanding empire, according to Muslim and non-Muslim scholars alike, was either spurious or put in circulation for specific purposes. Consequently, accurate reports had to be distinguished from false ones. Moreover, there was much variation across the islands of Muslim communities across the empire with respect to what exactly constitutes the *Sunna* (the path, or the notion of what Islam is) since different bodies of authoritative sources would often be invoked. Muslims all shared the *Quran*, but what they referenced as the *hadith* varied; there were internal contradictions and substantial proportions were spurious. The idea that what Islam is could somehow vary across geographic regions prompted collective efforts to create the *Sunna* uniform and coherent. Because teaching of Islam had to be coherent, some two centuries after Mohammad's death, the collections of *hadith* were created and categorized by topic to obscure geographical differences. As a result, the *Sunna* ended with six collections of the *hadith* for *Sunnis* and four for *Shiites*.

The contradictions in the *hadith* were even more important in resolving disputes brought before the caliphs and the governors they appointed. Even a trustworthy report on a particular situation could not directly resolve most new legal problems that arose later. As the importance of law grew simultaneously with the growth of the community, questions arose about what to do (how to adjudicate) under particular circumstances. To address such problems, one possibility was to reason by analogy (*qiyas*) from one situation to another. Another was to reach communal (community) consensus (*Ijma*).[29] But at issue was also how to interpret the law from a variety of sources. Who would be able to determine how the sources of law fit together? In response to the increasing number of these dilemmas, in the 800s, groups of pious men embarked on the study and elaboration of norms as a religious activity. They did so by interpreting textual sources and applying a complex set of rules. The ones who especially trained in mastering doctrine and got involved in transmitting it came to be known as the scholars (*ulamma*). By analyzing, discussing, applying, and discovering laws, they were in a position to say how the sources of law fit together.

By combining legal and religious authority, the *ulamma* provided some uniformity to doctrine and the law derived from it.[30] They elaborated theology and helped develop a comprehensive legal system, the *sharia*—a symbol to the Divine path—ostensibly a set of unchanging beliefs and principles that order life in accordance with God's will. As such, the *sharia* would eventually become a symbol of solidarity and commonality for Muslims around the world. To believing Muslims, it is something that has moral and metaphysical purpose. Yet the *sharia* is not an easily identifiable set of rules that can be mechanically applied. It lacks unity as its application depends greatly on its interpretations.[31] Although the *ulamma* extracted law (the Divine Will) from the *Quran* and the *Sunna* based on the same general principles (e.g., justice) the differences would emerge over conceptions of equity and public interest based on geographic and political context in which interpreter lived (i.e. from more to less conservative).

Starting with the early 800s, almost two dozen schools of legal thought developed and their influence stretched over particular regions under Islamic rule.[32] The schools of law differed, for example, over individual issues such as qualifications (who you can marry), maintenance of a life (what kind of maintenance and how long), and "ideological rivalries" among them would sometimes even lead to armed confrontations. Similar to the threat posed to the integrity of Islam by earlier proliferation and localization of the *hadith*, the multiplicity of schools of thought seemed to be destructive and eventually prompted collective efforts to reduce further differentiation. Thus by 1100, in the *Sunni* world, four dominant schools of thought emerged: *Shafi'i*, *Hanafi*, *Maliki*, and *Hanbali*. For the *Shiites*, who believe that the succession of power followed the prophet's lineage, the prophet had several successors who claimed extraordinary divine authority. Once they were gone, however, the *Shiite* scholars came to occupy a role very similar to that of their *Sunni* counterparts. And the dominant schools of thought that emerged among them were *Jafari* and *Zaydi*.

The variety of legal schools of thought in Islam often made western scholars describe Islamic law as lacking legal uniformity and having lax criteria for the jurisdiction of individual judges. But *sharia*, as discussed in the following section, played a key (political and legal) role in the preservation of the Muslim community and persisted to the recent day. Although belonging to a variety of schools of thought, the *ulamma* provided an important source of religious authority in the Muslim world. By interpreting a law that originated with God, they forced the caliphs to increasingly rely on their opinions and to acknowledge them as guardians of the *sharia* law.[33] In the middle of the ninth century, the division of authority became an enduring feature of Islamic societies.[34] This dispersal of religious authority actually created the separation of power in the Islamic state: The caliph had paramount responsibility to fulfill the divine injunction to "command the right and prohibit the wrong." It required him to delegate responsibility to scholarly judges, who would apply God's law as they interpreted it. In the classical age of Islam, judicial authority came from the caliph, but the law to be applied came from the scholars.[35] The state could not produce *sharia* law; only the jurists could do so.

The *Sharia* and the State
Balance of Power between the Ruler and the Scholars

Three defining features of the original Muslim political community of Medina were as follows: (1) a ruler's authority derived from divine right; (2) the ideal of good government extolling moral virtues of the ruler; (3) and the character of the ruler rather than the efficacy of his rule as a principle criterion for evaluating the caliph's competence. Given the emphasis on the ruler's piety and ethical considerations of his character in this conception of political community, there was little interest in how emerging administrative institutions of the expanding state might affect or shape moral conduct of the ruler. As the caliphate came to resemble the imperial (monarchical state), moral and governing actions increasingly found justification in utilitarian calculations and actions evaluated based on their consequences rather than on their intentions. Although consistently guided by a single religious faith, the solidarity of the *umma* became less dependent on a morally virtuous (ethical sphere) and individually pious (religious sphere) caliph and more dependent on his efficient administrative and military control of the expanding state. The solidarity eventually became dependent on an uneasy relationship between the temporal political power and the divine justification of spiritual authority in the state.

The *sharia* played a central role in maintaining the balance between the two. Adherence to the *sharia* was key to the preservation of the legal and political order; it had supremacy over all else. By interpreting a law that originated with God, the *ulama*, comprising theologians, intellectuals, and judges, have acquired the authority to bind the community to obedience—including the ruler. They were part of the political, legal, and judicial system. According to the concept of government developed by the scholars, the very purpose of the ruler was the enforcement of divine law. Breaking of the law would demonstrate that one was incompetent to rule (which is what kept the rulers within the bounds of law). Merely declaring the ruler subject to the law was not enough on its own; the ruler actually had to honor the law. The system of government provided him with an incentive to do so, in the form of a balance of power with the *ulama*. The ruler could naturally put pressure to get the desired results in particular cases but because the scholars were in charge of the law, and he was not, the ruler could abandon the course of justice only at the expense of being seen to violate God's law—thereby undermining the very basis of his rule. "Commanding good and forbidding evil was both the state's reason for being and the basis for the rulers' claim to be obeyed."[36] Theorists of classical Islam could thus assert that religion and political authority each depended upon the other.

But the authority of scholars over the rulers also extended to several other issues. They would affirm the initial legitimacy of the ruler who would either be appointed by the predecessors or elected by the small group of the inner circle. They would, as agents of stability (and predictability), also provide the continuing legitimacy to the caliph's rule and thus fend off potential challengers to the caliph's rule. Finally, they would help the caliph, by declaring the religious obligation to protect the state in a defensive *jihad*. Failure to act in accordance with the scholar's legal dictates was not supported by the *Quran*'s injunction to "obey those in authority among you" and could undermine the ruler's legitimacy.[37] The *sharia* thus guaranteed a balanced state in which legal rights were respected by the rulers. The traditional Islamic government of a state under *sharia* was, for more than a millenium, subject to a version of the rule of law that did not place rulers above the law. The *ulama* could limit the ability of the executive to expropriate the property of private citizens, induce the executive to rely on lawful taxation to raise revenues, and thus force the rulers to be responsive to their subjects' concerns. Authority originated from divine right and not a ruler's political right. Religion legitimated political action and authority and imposed a legally responsible order on the exercise of power. Thus, *sharia* was key to the continuing existence of Islamic society from its inception to the late nineteenth century.

The Integrity of the *Sharia* and the Breaks in the Continuity of the State

No temporal ruler could maintain absolute control of an empire that stretched from Morocco in Western Africa to the Indian subcontinent in South Asia. Even when the Abbasids were at the peak of their power, individual areas slipped away from Baghdad's authority and other Islamic dynasties began to develop. This process intensified following the rule of al-Mu'tasim and that of his son, al-Wathiq (842–847 AD), when the centralized power of the Abbasid caliphate started to decline. Thus in 756, the Umayyads, with the help of the Kharijite North Africans (especially the Berbers), established a rival empire in Spain. The survivors of the 786 Mecca massacre of Shi'ite 'Alid, fled to the western region of Africa (the Maghreb), and established an independent kingdom of the Idrisid. By early 800, Tunisia's governors carved out an area of governance of their own. As a result, Tunisia, Algeria, Morocco, and Spain had separated themselves from the caliphate. Similarly, southern Pakistan became an area independent of the caliphate. The decline in political authority also affected the core of the empire. So by 945, the area around Iraq fell to an Iranian military dynasty, the Buyids (Buwayhids), while from the tenth to the twelve centuries, the Fatimids, an Ismaili *Shia* dynasty, established the rule of Egypt, the Levant, and the heart of Saudi Arabia. In other words, after only two hundred years in power, the unified cultural and political world of Islam fragmented into a myriad of independent political units.

These changes in political realities raised the issues of continued spiritual authority and political legitimacy of the caliphate. Although the office of the caliphate remained with the Abbasid dynasty from 750 to 1258, starting with the latter part of the ninth century, the Abbasids were only figureheads. As the caliphs became powerless, they were still invested with theoretical legitimacy as the arbiters of any affairs concerning all Islam and as the source of authority to the various emirs.[38] However, the authority of the emirs rested primarily on their political power and only secondarily on their religious legitimacy. The relationship between the caliphate and the emerging emirates somehow had to be determined. In two specific instances it became necessary to reconcile traditional requirements of maintaining the caliph's primacy in governance. One was a situation in which, through the process of political fragmentation or by taking power through force, a local ruler (provincial governor) would refuse to obey orders from the political center and proclaim himself a ruler (rather than being designated initially by the caliph). Another was a situation of a foreign invasion, which would leave the caliph under control by a person who exercised executive authority (where the caliph would not be a de facto ruler).[39] Such a situation occurred after 1055 when Baghdad fell to Seljuk Turks challenging the caliphal throne of Harun al-Rashi.

Could a caliph be a caliph if he had no more than ritual power? Citing the necessity of preserving the social order, Abu al-Hasan al-Mawardi, (972–1058 CE), a theologian and scholar, provided justification of rule for both situations. So long as the de facto ruler followed the principles of religion and the sharia law, Mawardi argued, the caliph could allow the political rule to continue, allowing the authority of the caliphate to be preserved through legal fiction. In each of the two situations, there might have been reasons for the abolishment of the caliphate but this would have also implied the break in continuity of the law.[40] The preservation of the legal system (despite the change in political power), on the other hand, was crucial because of the public interest in preserving contracts, judgments, and property rights. The sharia therefore outlived the political and military decline of the caliphate, which had been designed to serve it. If the caliphate were to disappear, later argued another religious scholar, Abu Hamid al-Ghazali (1058–1111), the law itself would cease to operate. Al-Ghazali, who lived in Baghdad under the rule of the Seljuks—one of the rare groups that managed to reverse the process of steady decentralization of the political rule throughout the Muslim community of faith, argued that the preservation of the caliphate, in form if not in substance, was simply the necessity of preserving the legal system. According to him, the community of the faithful was enjoined to obey its ruler, not as interpreter but as a symbol of the continuity of the Muslim community, simply because the alternative was chaos.[41]

Al-Mawardi's and al-Ghazali's reasoning effectively marked a shift in justification of the caliphal rule from the one mainly in spiritual and ethical terms to the one in political and functional terms. The role of the caliph would no longer be that of interpreter; rather, it would be that of a symbol of continuity of the Muslim community. Henceforth, Muslim jurists reached a consensus regarding the test of the legitimacy of temporal rulers: as long as the ruler could defend the territories of Islam (*dar al-Islam*) and did not prevent his Muslim subjects from practicing their religion, the challenge to his political authority was unjustifiable. They claimed that anarchy (*fitna*) is worse than tyranny, since the former could threaten the disintegration of the *umma*. In their view, anarchy was the worst thing that could occur in human society because of what follows from the absence of the religious law. In order to enforce the religious law effectively there is a need for government. On that basis both *Sunnis* and *Shiites* agree that there should be a government in some form. The practice based on this particular reasoning, to a large extent, underlined the rule in most Muslim polities that until the eighteenth century would be described by some as a period of political quietism.[42]

The regional rulers sought to justify their positions within the Abbasid system, obtaining recognition of their positions from the caliph while simultaneously attempting to justify their rule on its own merits. Eventually the concept of the sultanate emerged. The title of sultan implied unrestricted sovereignty with caliphal certification, implying *Sunni* piety and rigor of *sharia* law.[43] Mahmud of Ghazna (ruled between 998 and 1030) was the first person to hold the title of sultan and the Seljuks were the first dynasty of sultans.[44] After the 1258 Mongol invasion and the subsequent fall of the Abassid caliphate, the principal political expression of Islam at the time, multiple centers of political power developed. In the newly formed emirates, ultimate control was in the hands of a supreme military ruler whose succession was determined by armed contest within the ruling dynasty.[45] In these efficient, highly organized states, largely based on the army, the rules of succession—either by appointment of the incumbent ruler or by the collective decision—were compromised while the spiritual leadership/guidance seemed to have been abandoned. The *ulama* were nevertheless inclined to grant at least some legitimacy to the emirs on the grounds that they provided the political order necessary for the preservation of the community.[46] As a result, the social unity of the *umma* and the norms that governed

Muslim life did not decline with the caliphate. This explains why in the sixteenth century the central Islamic lands that had been so devastated by the Mongol invasions recovered their political unity and cultural vitality, which gave rise to the Mughal Empire of Delhi in the east (1526–1764), the Ottoman Empire (1299–1923) in the west, and the Iranian Safavid Empire (1502–1736) in between.

The Mamluk kingdom, which had ruled Egypt and Syria between 1250 and 1517, maintained an Abbasid pretender in Cairo until the Ottoman conquest of Egypt that ended their rule. Mamluk control of pilgrim access to Mecca and Medina was key to their legitimacy, but Muslim rulers elsewhere rarely recognized their status as protectors of Islam.[47] The 1517 conquest of the Mamluk kingdom permitted the Ottomans to establish *suzerainty* over Mecca and Medina and allowed them to elevate their status from a peripheral to a central power in the Islamic world. Beginning with Suleiman the Magnificent (1520–66), however, the Ottoman sultans had themselves declared caliphs, notwithstanding the express constitutional requirement of Arab Qurashi descent, which they lacked. The Ottoman sultan would use a title "caliph," usually as a secondary one as the role of the caliph had been of lesser significance than the role of the protector of the holy cities of Mecca and Medina. As caliphs, the Ottomans theoretically assumed responsibility for preserving the *sharia*. In other words, they earned the caliphate at the price of accepting that God and his law were above them.[48] In return, the Ottomans could claim God-given sovereignty of a ruler responsible for the perpetuation of good order that requires absolute obedience in order to preserve social harmony.[49]

Ottoman policy of empire building was based on a belief in the ruler's responsibility for instituting and enforcing the laws and values of Islam.[50] The Ottoman sultans accepted their Islamic duties by implementing the *sharia*, and by establishing an Islamic legal system throughout the empire and an elaborate court tradition that endowed religious scholars with the monarch's patronage. In addition, the Ottomans assumed the role of protectors of the universal Islamic community, a role highlighted after they took over the administration of Jerusalem, Damascus, Baghdad, and the holy places of Mecca and Medina. But their rule also included pragmatic solutions of temporal power such as the explicit adoption of the notion of hereditary dynasty. As the Ottoman state evolved from a *gazi* principality to a bureaucratic world empire, the sultans instituted an imperial council, or divan, to deal with the increasingly complex affairs of government.

Sufism and *Sufi* Brotherhoods
Inward and Outward Manifestations of Islam

Sufism, or Islamic mysticism, began as a movement among individuals who opposed the worldliness and materialism of the Umayyad court in Damascus.[51] It developed as a protest against corrupt rulers who, according to *Sufis*, did not embody Islam. It was also a reaction to the legalism and formalism of worship, which paid more attention to the form rather than content of the faith. *Sufis* viewed the Islamic concept of *jihad* not as a war against the infidels but as a war against one's own defects—a war that a Muslim has to fight to try to reach perfection. It is an inward struggle for enlightenment, a practice toward inner awakening. In the Islamic context, this meant coming as close to God as Prophet Muhammad had done. From a theological point of view, *Sufism* was not a departure from Islam; rather, it was a different way of looking at the Islamic faith. Whereas the *ulama* practiced the formal intellectualism (oriented toward *sharia*), *Sufi* mystics, in an attempt to attain closer communion with God, centered on emotional religious experience. The fundamental nature of *Sufi* is that the person who has chosen this path can reach an individual contact with God. *Sufi* followers use a variety of techniques to move toward God, like singing, circular dances, etc. *Sufis* have a teacher who acts as an intermediary between God and the person and who gives the precepts according to which people should behave.

During the ninth century, *Sufism* evolved into a devotional movement that obtained a large following particularly in rural areas. Some *Sufis* became ascetics who gathered disciples around themselves and developed religious orders known as *dervishers*. Others forsook the orders and became mendicants, traveling around the countryside and living off the charity of others. Between the ninth and eleventh centuries, *Sufism* made a significant contribution to Islamic music, art, and architecture. Starting with the twelfth and thirteenth centuries, groups of *Sufis* who practiced the same ritual and followed the same master formed themselves into structured brotherhoods (*tariqahs*), which were bound by the oath of allegiance.[52] Down to the present day, *Sufi* brotherhoods practice some form of a sacred ceremony as a sacramental reenactment of the initiation offered by Prophet Muhammad to his companions. During the "taking hand" ceremony, as this act of initiation is called, the new dervish receives the blessings of the lineage and a promise of spiritual protection along his life's journey.

The brotherhoods that meet regularly in acts of collective piety are headed by a spiritual leader called a *shaykh*, who is considered the most spiritual man. *Shaykh's* authority is based on the idea that he was capable of, or had already achieved, some sense of (direct) awareness of proximity to God. The solemn moment of taking *bayat*, the Arabic word for an oath of loyalty, is the ritual of accepting the *shaykh* as guide and coming under the protection of the lineage of the order. *Bayat* means religious submission to a *shaykh* rather than personal allegiance to him and makes a *Sufi* connection possible in the chain that connects one to become a recipient of the light of Muhammad (saws). Brotherhoods practice their own rituals and their mystical or devotional ways (*tariqa*) according to the formula established by the founder of the particular order. Their spiritual exercises (*dhikr*) include reciting prayers and passages of the *Quran* and repeating the names, or attributes, of God while performing physical movements. The outcome of an exercise, which lasts much longer than the usual daily prayer, is often an ecstatic state. Besides offering spiritual fulfillment, the brotherhoods also mobilize people for communal volunteer activities.

The brotherhoods vary considerably in their practice and internal organization. Some orders are tightly organized in hierarchical fashion while others have allowed their local branches considerable autonomy. There is often tension between rival orders that sometimes undermine tribal loyalties. Although most brotherhood organizations were local, several of them established regional branches, and a few managed to set up networks throughout Africa or the Middle East. Their numbers spread so fast that by the1500s, it appears that a male belonged to at least one *Sufi* brotherhood. They came to Sudan in the sixteenth century and played an important part in the religious revival that swept through North Africa during the eighteenth and nineteenth centuries. The brotherhoods flourished everywhere but particularly on the periphery of the Muslim world. The Tijaniyah (*Tijaniyya*) Order, founded in Morocco by Ahmad at-Tijani in 1781, extended the borders of Islam toward Senegal and Nigeria, and their representatives founded large kingdoms in West Africa.

This same order is associated with the Muslim Brotherhood, which began in Egypt in the late 1920s and later spread throughout the Arab world. *Sufi* brotherhoods often put premium on the organizations themselves and ignored national boundaries.

Unlike *ulama* who had knowledge of religion but little capacity (in most cases) to influence the political sphere, *Sufi* brotherhoods possessed that capacity. As a result, the brotherhoods have traditionally played an important role in mobilizing Muslim populations against occupying forces. For example, a *Sufi* brotherhood was instrumental in organizing an opposition to the French colonial rule in Morocco in the 1830s. The leader of the revolt, Abdul Kadar (the Algerian), was the leader of the Kadaria *Sufi* brotherhood, an international political force influential in remote corners of the Muslim world such as Indonesia, and which played an important role in mobilizing Muslims against the Soviet Union in Afghanistan. Similarly, Sheikh Amadou Bamba (1853–1927), the spiritual leader of some four million Muslims in Senegal, was a *Sufi* who resisted French colonial oppression through pacifism. A *Sufi* brotherhood is still potent today in Sudan where some of the major political figures are descendants of Mahdi (a leader of the movement discussed in the following section).

Sufis tended to be tolerant of local cultures and customs; they often fused Islamic practices with pre-Islamic cultural forms.[53] *Sufism*, which makes use of paradigms and concepts derived from Greek, Hindu, and other non-Islamic sources, is generally less concerned with reinforcing and defending religious boundaries than the *Sunni* establishment regularly is. Moreover, the *Sufi* doctrine of "the unity of being," has inclined *Sufis* to emphasize interiority and the oneness of humanity, often at the expense of official *Sunni* Islam and its insistence on the conformity of the external world of state and society to *sharia*. The *Sufi* emphasis on Islam's mystical tradition emphasized the direct knowledge, personal experience, and spiritual sovereignty of God, all of which were at odds with the *Sunni* establishment and its dedication to enforcing the legal and political sovereignty of Allah. *Sufis's* reverence of saints, as well as their use of music and dance to connect with the divine, brought them into conflicts with Orthodox *Sunni* Muslim theologians who viewed strong mystical components of *Sufism* as heresy. Puritanist, non-*Sufi* Muslim groups regard the *Sufis* as being involved in innovating, or placing human figures between man and God, which they say challenges monotheism. Muslim scholars claimed that *Sufi* brotherhoods represented superstition and that they should be weeded out.

Chapter 3

Religious Revivalism, Literalism, and Fundamentalism

The earlier section has already established that for practicing Muslims abandoning Muhammad's model of community amounted to renunciation of God. To many, scattered throughout the areas under Muslim rule, innovations in the models of communal governance in the name of greater administrative efficacy, adoption of non-Bedouin customs, the separation of the sultanate and the caliphate, and the localization of charisma, each discussed in the previous sections, appeared as deviant departures from the original precepts of the *Quran*. Some religious opposition would come from the *ulama*. However, throughout the history of the Islamic civilization, various groups formed in order to restore religious purity or moral conservatism. The Khartijities, and the challenges they posed to the Umayads and their political power was discussed in the earlier section. The Abbasids successfully replaced the Ummayads (in 750 AD) by claiming that their secular-minded predecessors betrayed the spirit of Islam. The major thrust of Islamic political theory and practice has continued in the direction charted by Mawdardi and Ghazali; that is, the religious establishment worked closely with the executive body in the state. But this relationship was not without tensions and the doctrinal-based Islamic revivalists continued to reappear.

While the political theory and practice advocated by Mawdardi and Ghazali gave primacy to the preservation of the legal system and provided a functional justification of political power, for Ahmad Ibn Taymiyya (1268–1328), another important scholar of Islamic law and theology, and an important political figure of his time, the departure from the precepts of early Islam led to an illegitimate rule. Ibn Taymiyya lived during one of the most disruptive periods of Islamic history, which had seen the fall of Baghdad and the conquest of the Abbasid Empire in 1258 by the Mongols. Reacting to the Mongols' occupation and to what he perceived as subsequent immoral rule, Ibn Taymiyya preached that Islam justified the right to rebel against unjust rulers.[1] He called on a rigorous, literalist interpretation of the sacred sources for the crucially needed Islamic renewal and reform of his society.[2]

During the eighteenth and nineteenth centuries, an increase in doctrinally based Islamic movements occurred among the rural populations in various Islamic regions.[3] The three most influential movements were the Sanusi order in Libya, the Mahdiwah movement in Sudan, and the Wahhabi movement on the Arabian Peninsula. "In contrast to prior periods when Islamic revivalism occurred in a specific empire or region, eighteenth-century movements extended from modern-day Sudan, Libya, and Nigeria, across the Arabian Peninsula and the Indian subcontinent to Southeast Asia."[4]

The Sanusi movement rejected the Ottoman and Egyptian forms of Islamic behavior in favor of a more austere desert life seeking to recreate the original community of the Prophet. Al-Sanusi integrated the surrounding tribes into his religious order and established a comprehensive network of brotherhoods and trading posts stretching from northern Cyreniaca into the Sudan. The late nineteenth century Mahdiyyah uprising in the northern Sudan was both a rebellion against the Egyptian occupation of the Sudan and a movement for the purification of Islam (a program of moral reform not just for Sudan but for all of Islam). Claiming an inspiration from God, Muhammad Ahmad (1844–1885) of the *Sufi* background, in 1881 proclaimed himself the Mahdi, the expected one. His goal was the revival of the faith and practice of the Prophet through the restoration of the *Quran* and the *hadith* as the foundations of a just society. Al-Sanusi made a virtue of the poverty of the Sudan by renouncing worldly goods and citing the relative luxury of the Egyptian governors as evidence of their impious behavior. He formed a state, modeled closely on the Prophet's practice in Medina, and appointed his own caliph. He further declared a *jihad* against the Egyptian administration, claiming that only by dislodging these lax Muslims from the Sudan could a true Islamic society be established. In 1885, the Mahdi attracted a large and devoted following and conquered most of the northern Sudan, including the future capital city of Khartoum.

Of all revivalist movements at the time, by far the greatest impact on the future of Islam would have been the Wahhabi (Unitarian or Mywahhidun) movement on the Arabian Peninsula.[5] Driven by his idiosyncratic interpretations of Islam, Muhammad Ibn Abd al-Wahhab (1703–1792) rejected the variety of schools of thought and adopted the strict, austere *Hanbali* law as superior to the other three sanctioned schools of law. His writing criticized the beliefs and customs of the Najdis in the Arabian Peninsula, where social relations were organized on the basis of a customary code and parts of Islamic law were fused with local traditions. He pushed for a greater influence of the orthodox *ulama*, and after his stay in Medina, began articulating his opposition to what he saw as non-Islamic aspects of Muslim life. His main concern was purity of religion rather than unity of the Muslim community. Al-Wahhab gave primacy to the sacred texts and as a fundamentalist reformer distinguished himself by an approach that reflected total rejection of *Sufism* and hostility to *Shiism*.[6]

Al-Wahhab's alternative called for a return to adopting the correct beliefs and practices mandated by God. This implied the restoration of a genuinely Islamic society that would be modeled after the Prophet's city-state in Medina and the precedents of the "Rightly Guided" early generations (*al-salaf al-salih*). He called for a return to the pure, refined faith and practice, to what he perceived as the only true path.[7] He insisted that the *Quran* and the *Sunna* were the only reliable sources through which the divine will could be comprehended. Yet, his return to the fundamentals of the faith mistook Arab culture for the universal precepts of Islam; it confused the imperative of social unity with social uniformity (a single way to live). Al-Wahhab and his followers seem to have been driven by the "old ethocentric belief that only Arabs (the pure Arab culture, the Bedouin culture of the Najd region), can represent the one true and authentic Islam."[8] Although the power of the Wahhabi forces was broken by the Egyptian forces, led by Ibrahim Ali, the reformist ideal of Abd al-Wahhab became ingrained among the tribes of Arabia and would later play a significant role in the creation of the state of Saudi Arabia.

PART TWO
Modernization, Nationalism, and State Building

Chapter 4

Islam and the Philosophy of the Enlightenment

Driven by historical conditions unique to Europe, the eighteenth-century Enlightenment ushered in rationalism and removed religious belief as the touchstone of human life. Reason separated from the divine made religion one of several competing points of view. It undermined the ability of Christian churches, Catholic and Protestant alike, to claim a monopoly on interpretation of the physical world and to maintain their key role in guiding human life. As science separated from theology, so did moral and legal norms. A new tradition emerged, one with an opportunity for justification of moral and legal actions independent of theological doctrines. By virtue of being separated from religious doctrine, law lost its permanence; it was no longer developed by interpretation of the divine will, but instead expressed the will of a sovereign lawgiver that became open to revision.[1] As legal norms became subjected to criticism and in need of rational public justification, a new public sphere was created as a conduit between society and state. In the absence of "religious unity" of thought and religious justification of norms, it became possible to hold public discussions on the exercise of political power, eventually facilitating political pluralism.

By the 1800s, religious laws in northwestern and central Europe had been abandoned and increasingly replaced by civil legal codes, and secular schools outnumbered the religious ones. In a changing worldview, motives came to matter less than the consequences of actions. As legality of individual actions became a basis of accountability, the attribution of moral intention became less relevant in the legal system. Similarly, the issue of legitimacy of political governance, having been detached from the divine, became generated by legality leading to a notion of the legal basis of political power.[2] Putting these ideas into practice, the American and French revolutions have undermined legitimacy of a divinely ordained, hierarchical, dynastic realm, and replaced it with the concept of popular sovereignty.

The Enlightenment thus introduced profound changes in the legal and political theory and practice but was initially geographically confined to Northwestern Europe—England, Scotland, northern France, and Germany—and did not become an immediate success. The turn to popular sovereignty, in continental Europe at least, had initially been stalled and reversed (most notably in France). Nevertheless, the idea of a constitutional secular state, with a public sphere open to legislative and political debates, started taking hold in north and central Europe towards the last decades of the nineteenth century. A transition from communities of faith to national communities created universal citizenship and territorial patriotism, markedly reduced the role of religion in education, and virtually eliminated its traces in the judiciary and the legal system. It called for a relationship between government and citizens that imposed limits on the rulers. At the same time, a new model of a centralized state started to develop in Europe. It was one that promoted cultural uniformity, elaborate bureaucracy, a unified legal system, a strong executive power, and changes in the military and the fiscal system. The awareness of highly centralized but constitutional and secular states gradually reached the regions outside of northwestern and central Europe.

Some in the Middle East, most notably the educated elites, either schooled in Europe or by Europeans, had been exposed to these reformist ideas. The influence of the Enlightenment ideas had intensified particularly with the French military involvement in North Africa (Algeria, Tunisia, and Egypt). In the core of the Ottoman Empire, however, Islam was central to the Ottoman Empire and the *sharia* continued to be essential to the legal and political system. Religion was both an anchor for a community of faithful and a mechanism for the rule of an empire. It was at the roots of the social and economic basis of power as well as the substance of the legitimating ideology of the state. The *sharia* played a role both in the legal systems and in a system of governance. Unlike the church in Europe, the mosque in the Ottoman Empire was not an alternative and competitive institution to the state; it was dependent for its existence on the state. It worked within the state, rather than outside of and opposed to it. Islam, particularly as a legal system, was still believed to be universal and effective. In the *Sunni* Muslim community, religious law was the most important law; it had been regarded as just in the sense that it did not discriminate against religious minorities or non-privileged classes. This had been in part a result of the theory of Islamic law but perhaps even more importantly of the way the courts operated. In sum, the *sharia* had been regarded as just and was universally applied. Its implementation, as part of the legal tradition discussed in the earlier sections, also prevented tyranny of the political rule.

Chapter 5

The *Tanzimat* Reforms in the Ottoman State

At its base, the Ottoman state was composed of small-scale, local communities unified by religious affiliation and organized and identified in lineage, tribal, and ethnic terms (both in Arab and non-Arab provinces). The Ottomans tolerated a rich diversity of religious and cultural practices; they directly governed the areas that could be efficiently controlled (e.g., in Anatolia) and allowed a certain degree of latitude to chieftains and feudal emirs in more remote locations. Even in areas of direct control (as in Greater Syria), the Ottoman governors often exercised their authority in association with the local Arab notables. As the economic and military posture of the Ottoman Empire weakened in the course of the eighteenth century, an opportunity was created for provincial cities (e.g., Cairo and Baghdad) and warlords on the fringes of the Empire to become even more autonomous from the military and political center. The gradual erosion of political power in the Ottoman state soon prompted reforms that sought primarily to restructure the military and centralize the administration of the state. This was the beginning of "modernization"—of doing something that resembled the processes of state centralization and bureaucratization in central and northwestern European described above—driven primarily by internal needs of the empire.[1]

Modernization of the Ottoman military started under Sultan Selim III (reigned 1789–1807) and Sultan Mahmud II (reigned 1808-1839), both of whom dealt with rival centers of power by trying to establish more centralized governing structures with a new army loyal to the state. But the modernization of the military was also taking place, and at the faster pace, in the Ottoman province of Egypt. By buying wheat from Egyptian producers cheaply and selling it at high profit margins internationally, the Egyptian leader Mohammad Ali was able to enlarge immensely the treasury of the provincial government, which allowed him to entirely reshape Egypt's military. With the abundance of state funds, he built arms factories and developed military schools (for artillery) and soon made Egypt so powerful that in 1839 it threatened the Ottoman Sultan's rule in Syria. Only the coordinated Russo-British intervention prevented Egypt's eastern expansion at the expense of the Ottomans.

Obvious vulnerability of the empire prompted the next Ottoman leader, Rashid Pasha, to introduce more systematic, so-called *Tanzimat* (the Turkish word for reorganization, renewal or re-ordering) reforms in 1839. Leaders of the *Tanzimat* reforms were high military officials, civil servants, and writers—all with strong European connections and mostly influenced by French culture.[2] The reforms had various dimensions—political, legal, economic, and educational—but were apparently relatively slow initially and not thorough enough, as they were unable to slow down further erosion of the military and political power of the empire. The Ottomans soon avoided another military defeat, this time from the Russian forces in the 1856 Crimean War, only after the joint Franco-British intervention, while in 1861 the Tunisian province successfully broke away from the Ottoman rule. As a concession to the British and the French after the Crimean War, the Ottomans granted equality to all citizens and started the process of political reforms that eventually led to the 1876 constitution and the elected parliament. Much of the impetus for the intensification of the *Tanzimat* reforms thus came from British and French pressures.

Although the Islamic foundations of society were not openly questioned by the new generation of Western-trained officials, their policies tended to reduce the significance of the religious establishment and to enhance the opportunities available to individuals trained as they were. The state-established military schools were meant to strengthen the army and the state. Since the underlining rationale for modern education was service to the state, nearly all of the military school graduates expected to be employed by the government. That was an objective significantly different from more numerous religious schools devoted to Islam. Higher-level *madrasas* taught Islamic law and religious studies, preparing students for jobs in education and law rather than specifically for the government jobs.

On the economic front, the Ottoman state experienced a growing external debt to the European lenders. The penetration of European merchant capital into the empire brought about a shortage of raw materials for domestic consumption, whereas the growing domestic demand for imports caused the suffering of local handicraft industries. Inefficient taxation based on special concessions and patronage led to a decline of state revenues; in order to cover its annual budget deficits, the empire began to take out loans from the European money markets.[3] As a result, by 1874, about 60 percent of the state's total expenditure was devoted to servicing debt, which in effect made the Ottoman Empire bankrupt. As the Ottoman government effectively surrendered its financial independence to European interests, Western powers could put additional political pressures for speeding up the reforms.[4] In addition to making significant changes in education, the Ottoman state now secularized the judiciary and the legal system, and nationalized religious properties and endowments, further reducing the sociopolitical role of religion in the process.[5]

The marginalization of the religious establishment was not simply a side effect of reforms and restructuring in the Ottoman state. It was a concerted effort of the government to more directly and more pervasively insert the central state into the daily lives of its subjects than had previously been the case. It did so in order to expand governmental control and administration and eliminate intermediaries between the population and the state, particularly the religious scholars and the *millet* religious leaders of minority religious groups.[6] By the late nineteenth century, the Ottoman state, similar to the political practices developed in France decades earlier, adopted a policy that made religion subordinate to the secular structure of governance. Based on this policy, the religious scholars would receive a salary from the state, while its domain of action would be regulated by the laws of the land. Naturally, the religious Islamic establishment opposed the far-reaching reforms that progressively weakened its social status and influence. Since the scholars became the principal source of political opposition, the state's primary objective was to try to minimize their role in public affairs. It did so in a series of measures including the elimination of their financial independence, the codification of the law, and the promotion of the concept of citizenship.

The *Ulama*'s Loss of Financial Independence

An adminsitrative structure in the religious establishment of the Ottoman Empire started with *sheyk al-Islam* at the top, followed by separate chief judges for Europe and Asia and then further down by judges, muftis, and jurist councils. In terms of their financial dependence on the state, two categories of religious officials were distinguished. While the elite class of religious leadership, those with the roles in the religious administration directly under the *sheyk al-Islam*, were salaried employees of the state, the bulk of the money that went to the lower ranked *ulama* did not come from the state treasury or taxation. Rather, it was based on the institution of *waqf* (a religious trust, foundation)—a gift of a pious person of substantial value. Over the centuries, the *waqf* system developed into a central institution in Muslim societies, providing welfare and educational benefits to a large segment of the population. It led to the accumulation of religiously endowed landed property so that by the late nineteenth century the *waqf* systems controlled almost three-quarters of the agricultural land in the Ottoman Empire.[7]

Before the advanced stages of the *Tanzimat* reforms, the *ulama* played a central role in managing the *waqf* system. But the government increasingly regarded this institution as an obstacle to the consolidation of the state power and eventually made its nationalization as one of its principal targets in the process. It insisted on the backwardness of the *waqf* system, stressing its inefficient management and rigidity in the face of changing social and economic conditions. Resistant to market forces, the government claimed, the *waqf* system locked vast resources into unproductive organizations responsible for delivering social services. The government's centralizing efforts in the late nineteenth century therefore sought to break the hold of the *ulama* over *waqfs* and to gain control of the revenues generated by these endowments.[8] It called for the system to be reformed and centrally controlled by the government, or perhaps even to be abolished entirely. As early as 1826, the government decreed that the *waqf* settled in the land of the Ottoman Empire be put under the supervision of a new imperial Ministry of *Waqf* justifying its new policy by claiming that *waqf* revenues should not be left in the hands of dubious property administrators (*mutawallis*). This new policy opened the way of nationalization of vast *ulama*-controlled properties.[9]

An even more serious damage to the *waqf* system came with the *Tanzimat* reforms in 1863 when the state introduced numerous administrative requirements that basically discouraged the foundation of new *waqfs*. In Egypt the central administration of *waqf* properties began under Muhammad Ali's rule in 1851 was later, in 1913, formalized by the establishment of a separate ministry for that particular purpose. State treasury officials, rather than *waqf* trustees now collected the donations from peasants, leaving only a certain percentage for the collections of *waqf* administrators. As the state allocated share to the *waqf* administrators decreased over time, the relationship between the Ministry of Finance and the *waqf* system administrators deteriorated. By administering gradual nationalization of the *waqfs*, the state reformers denied the *ulama* an economic base and effectively ended financial independence of a significant segment of the religious establishment similar to the processes of dispossession of the clerics in the English and French revolutions in the seventeenth and eighteenth centuries respectively.

Codification of Law

Besides the nationalization of the *waqf* system, the marginalization of the *ulama* continued to occur in education, albeit slowly. By 1876, secular education was still largely restricted to the military schools, while religious education continued to be relatively strong. That started to change only after 1876 when the state began to establish a number of secular, western-style, secondary schools. Much more severe restriction of the institutional role of the *ulama* came from the changes in law when the succession of Ottoman sultans promulgated the law codes borrowed (often almost verbatim) from the European legal systems. A global empire with a strong central administration needed an effective and unified secular legal system to keep its house in order and ensure the integrity of its economic system. The government established a system of secular courts called *nizame* to deal with cases involving both Muslims and non-Muslims, introduced new penal and commercial codes, and using the French civil code as a model compiled the sixteen-volume *Mejelle*.

The *Majelle* codification was inspired by and based on the *sharia*; it ensured that no matter how much Western law might affect commercial or maritime codes, the civil code of the empire remain within an Islamic framework. At the same time, the *Majelle*'s codification and the administration of the law were placed under the jurisdiction of a newly created Ministry of Justice. As the law increasingly came within the scope of the state, it gradually lost much of the autonomy it traditionally had, whereas the scholars were largely independent interpreters and practitioners unless they were involved with the judicial system of the state.[10] As the *sharia* became a set of rules defined and applied by authority of the state, the scholars lost their largely autonomous status of protectors of the law and became instead dependent state functionaries. The *sharia* courts continued to exist, but since their jurisdiction was confined to the areas of personal status and *waqfs*, the *ulama*'s legal activity was severely restricted. Instead, European-trained judges and lawyers came to dominate the system of justice and applied legal codes derived from European law. Reduced to "a set of subordinate legal rules" the *sharia* became less important in a judicial, legal system, and the system of governance.[11] By being marginalized in the legal system, the scholars also ceased to be necessary in providing legitimacy to political succession in government and justification of political rule.

Universal Citizenship

As the loyalty to the state and its secular structures grew in importance, the promulgation of new symbols of national identity became necessary. The adoption of nationalism was yet another way of separating the institutions of the state from religion. Modern citizenship called for a common Ottoman national identity that, in theory, would replace the religious ordering of society in which Muslims played a dominant role. In an effort to deemphasize religious affiliation and develop a sense of Ottoman citizenship, the Ottoman government issued two decrees (in 1839 and 1856) aiming especially at limiting the autonomy of non-Muslim religious groups (Greek Orthodox, Armenian Christians, and Jews), the so-called *millets*. The *millets* were directly administered by their own communal officials who exercised both civil and religious responsibilities including tax collection, education, justice, and religious affairs. In matters of civil conflict among members of the same *millet*, the conflict would be resolved by the traditional authorities and processes of the respective *millet*. So, for example, a Christian would be governed by Christian laws in his dealings with Christians, regardless of his personal location in the Ottoman Empire.[12]

The efforts to replace religious affiliation with secular identity continued with the proclamation of a Nationality Law in 1869.[13] But the concept of particularistic nationalism of the Ottoman state was difficult to reconcile with the universal nature of Islam. Although, according to the teachings of the *Quran*, God had created different people, Islam as a faith was for everyone. That made it difficult for a Muslim to distinguish national identity from a more universal Islamic identity. Whereas in Christianity or Judaism, given the tradition of local jurisdictions of religious institutions, it was possible to distinguish a national church or a patriarchy; in Islam it was much more difficult to disentangle the universalizing aspects of religion from the cultural particularity associated with a nation. This explains why, initially, in the last few decades of the nineteenth century there was no Egyptian, Albanian, or Syrian nationalism. While Turkish nationalists talked about *vatan* (fatherland in Turkish, analogous to the European notion of fatherlands) Arabs did not.[14] Pan-Ottomanism, an attempt to foster a European-style secular nationalism to integrate the multi-ethnic, religiously diverse, and disintegrating empire, was abandoned, if temporarily, after the ascent of the Ottoman Sultan Abdul Hamid II (1876–1909).[15]

Chapter 6

Kemalism: The Rule of Mustafa Kemal Ataturk

On the eve of the First World War, the governance of the Ottoman state fell into the hands of the Committee of the Union of Progress (CUP). The Young Turks, as this group came to be called informally, continued with the secular reforms of their predecessors. It abolished the *millet* system entirely, stressed the commitment to the preservation of the state based on Ottoman citizenship, and elevated the role of the military in the state. Whereas the *Tanzimat* reformers drew their inspiration from the French culture and focused mostly on legal and institutional reforms in the state, the Young Turks made considerable efforts to further strengthen the loyalty to the military as the principal agency of the state. By drawing from the German model of the organization of the military, the model that proved successful in Germany's rise to the status of a major European military power in the latter part of the nineteenth century, the Young Turks managed to instill a culture of strong loyalty to the state and the notion of the military as the privileged class in society.[1] Yet the CUP could not abandon the Islamic foundation on which imperial legitimacy rested for so many centuries.[2] The CUP regime had little choice but to continue to stress the role of the sultan as caliph and to use Islamic symbols to buttress its own claim to legitimacy.

This duality of secularizing legal reforms and religious sources of legitimacy would be maintained throughout the First World War. On the one hand, the war helped accelerate the secular transformation of the Ottoman social order. With large numbers of men mobilized for military service, more women were entering both the civil service of the state and the mainstream professions. Recognizing the changing circumstances, the CUP passed a legislation that made significant changes in the laws regulating family and personal status, the last important areas of jurisdiction still held by the religious establishment.[3] New secular authority was emphasized in those sections of the law recognizing the right of women to initiate divorce and restricting the grounds for the practice of polygamy. At the same time, in an effort to rally the Muslim population of the empire to the cause of the war and to arouse Muslim opinion against Britain and France, the CUP government mobilized the Islamic symbols. In November 1914, the sultan-caliph issued a call to *jihad*, urging Muslims the world over to unite behind the Ottoman Empire.[4]

As the war's end brought about the defeat and the subsequent fragmentation of the Ottoman Empire, the issue of legitimacy of the rump state came to the surface. For centuries, the Ottoman rulers had secured their legitimacy by guaranteeing a stable government, the political and social order based on the enforcement of *sharia* law, a respect for the role of the *ulama*, the patronage of religious education, and the protection of the holy cities of Mecca and Medina. By the end of the nineteenth century, as discussed above, the role of *sharia* law and its interpreters, the *ulama*, had been significantly reduced, whereas religious education had increasingly been replaced by the secular one. In the course of the war, the shrinking state lost its control over the two holy cities and the government scrambled to maintain the territorial integrity of the state's core. The war undermined the entire basis of the Ottoman system, effectively ending the social, political, and, significantly, religious order that had existed since the mid-fifteenth century.

What kind of cultural identity would replace the Ottoman imperial one? There were also open questions of political loyalty and succession. As a result of being partitioned and occupied in 1920, the Ottoman heartland of Anatolia emerged three years later as the internationally recognized independent nation-state of Turkey, free of restrictions on its domestic policies, on its finances, and on its jurisdiction over foreign nationals. In the world of emerging nation-states, the successor Turkish Republic sought to establish its legitimacy by claiming to represent a coherent national group, namely the Turks.[5] Turkish ethnicity was thus substituted for Islam as the means by which the nation-state was legitimated. The discussion of a Turkish cultural heritage as distinct from the Ottoman one, and as making crucial contribution to the successes of the empire, sowed the seeds for a Turkish nationalist movement in the postwar era.

In a number of significant ways, the CUP regime at the tail end of the *Tanzimat* reforms shaped the society in which sweeping reforms of Kemal Mustafa "Ataturk" would emerge at the end of the First World War. By shifting away from Islam as the foundation of the state, Ataturk combined commitment to modernization and Turkish nationalism to create the ideological underpinnings of the state. He viewed modern civilization as the one of only relevance in the contemporary world and endorsed rationality and science. Rather than seeing modernization as an import from abroad, he saw the Ottoman Turkish core as being essential in promoting it. Since Turkism, in his view, was the very source of modern civilization, becoming modern meant regaining identity that the Turks have actually already had. On the other hand, claiming that being Turk was superior to being of any other nationality, he elevated Turkish identity as a touchstone of the new state. In an effort to promote nationalism, with clear racial connotations, Ataturk sought to distance the Turkish identity from that of the Arabs. Claiming the superiority of Turkish over Arabic, Ataturk commissioned a translation of the *Quran* into Turkish and had it read publicly in 1932. That same year, the legislation made obligatory the issuing of the call to prayer in Turkish instead in Arabic.[6]

In line with this vision, the new state, in a relatively short period of time, promulgated national sovereignty as a legal basis of power, undertook sweeping institutional reforms, and promoted secular socialization. In 1922, the national assembly first passed a resolution that formally separated the caliphate from the sultanate. Soon thereafter, it eliminated the sultanate and initially made the office of the caliph of Islam subject to selection by a democratically elected body of national delegates. Finally, in 1924, the new Turkish constitution asserted the principles of republicanism and popular sovereignty and abolished the institution of the caliphate. The Turkish constitution further eliminated the office of *shaikh al-Islam* (a title of superior authority in the issues of Islam in the old regime) and the Ministry of Religious Endowments and called for the closing of religious schools, asserting instead the principle of free and compulsory secular education. In 1926, the Turkish assembly formally abolished the *Mejelle* and the *sharia* and adopted a Swiss civil code that forbade polygamy and broadened even further the grounds by which wives could seek divorce. The assembly also adopted penal and commercial codes modeled on Italian and German examples respectively. These institutional changes were complemented by policies of secular socialization aimed at molding the individual as a prelude to carrying out successful social change and development (e.g., the 1925 ban of wearing a fez).

Overall, the policies introduced in Turkey in the first half of the 1920s marked a clearly anti-religious doctrine. Ataturk's doctrine did not simply want to take religious affairs out of the hands of the scholars and put them in the hands of the laity. The Turkish government effectively took control over religious affairs by setting up the Ministry of Religious Affairs that became involved in making key appointments in the religious establishment. This radical secular doctrine based on the belief that there is no need for religion in public affairs allowed religion to exist only as a source of personal faith wholly subordinated to the state and made the military the guarantor of this new political order. The *ulama*, the judges, and the muftis continued to exist. But they were no longer regarded as part of the overarching, centralized administrative structure of religious authority as they once had been in the Ottoman regime.

Chapter 7

Arab Cultural Identity
and the New System of Nation-States

In contrast to the Ottoman European provinces (e.g., Greece, Serbia, and Romania), there was no distinct nationalism in the Arab-speaking parts of the empire prior to the twentieth century. As long as the empire satisfied the expectations of its subjects that the best interests of Islam (the ties of the *umma* were paramount) have been protected, most Arab Muslims accepted the legitimacy of the Ottoman rule.[1] The provinces of Egypt, Iraq, and Tunisia enjoyed various levels of political autonomy under the Ottoman rule. However, although in each of them, native populations spoke Arabic, the ruling classes were often non-Arabs. For example, in Egypt the ruling elites were composed of Turks, Circassians, and Albanians; whereas in Tunisia the members of the military elite were mostly of Turkish descent. The Arab provinces all shared the same religion, but the role of religion, much like in the core of the Ottoman Empire, had diminished by the changes at the governmental level that sought to marginalize the traditional scholars of religion. At the same time, to the Arab-speaking Ottoman provinces, cultural and political specificities of their locales seemed more important than any notion of their common Arab identity.

When Arab nationalists looked for common roots, they could find no single political historical narrative that would help broader social mobilization. They also lacked a geographic nucleus on which the future state of Arabs would be built upon, given that the Arab-speaking population was dispersed throughout the empire. The nationalists drew instead from the narrative of common cultural heritage and initiated the process of Arab awakening (*al nahdah*) whose principal aim was the promotion of the works in the Arabic language. Numerous other ambiguities remained. For example, given the size of the Arabic-speaking Christian community in Egypt and the large Arabic-speaking Jewish communities in Iraq, Yemen, and Morocco, it was difficult to think of the Arab cultural awakening as primarily Muslim in nature. Some of its leading figures were indeed Christians and Jews. The question was also to what extent was this awakening inspired by genuine local developments, since the institutions mostly involved in producing chief protagonists of the movement were predominantly non-Muslim, such as the Jesuit University of Saint Joseph in Beirut (established in 1875), the American Universities of Beirut (1866) and Cairo (1919), or the Alexandria based British prep school for the elites, the Victoria College.[2]

Early nationalism in Egypt, in particular, was not ethno-linguistic (neither Arab nor Egyptian) in its origin; it was primarily driven by the desire for independence from the British rule. Similarly, in Algeria the independence movement developed in opposition to the French administration and was not necessarily driven by the desire to create an Algerian national state. Among some of the Arab intellectuals there were also relatively strong feelings against the Ottoman control of the caliphate and the decadence brought upon Islam by the practices of Turks and other non-Arabs. Most prominently, a Syrian reformer, Abd al-Rahman al Kawakibi (1854–1902), tied Islam to the culture of its origin and suggested that the Ottomans were responsible for the corruption of Islam. He claimed that the virtues of Islam—its language, its Prophet, and its early moral and political order—were all Arab achievements. By glorifying the Arab role in the development of Islamic civilization, he called for the Ottomans to relinquish their unjustified claim to the caliphate and restore the office to its rightful possessors, the Arabs. In this view, the regeneration of Islam would begin with the establishment of an Arab caliph in Mecca whose responsibilities would be confined to purely religious matters.

An impetus for Arab political nationalism came with the onset of the First World War when the British, by taking advantage of the parallel Ottoman-Arab governing structures over the holy cities of Mecca and Medina, encouraged Arabs to rebel against the Ottoman rule, promising the creation of the Arab caliphate in return. In addition to the Ottoman governor of the sacred cities, the city of Mecca was also governed by a local governor of Mecca—a *sharif*. This was a person of great prestige, a figure informally subordinate to the Ottoman sultan but with a capacity, in theory if not in practice, to act as an independent authority. In a *sharif* of Mecca, British officials found a dignitary who could possibly ally with the Entente powers in the First World War (e.g., France, Great Britain, and Russia) and thus serve as a counterweight to the prestige of the Ottoman sultan-caliph, a formal war enemy. The creation of a state in Arabia was thus in the British interest to further weaken the Ottoman Empire. It was also in the interest of some Arab opinion leaders who had hoped for self-governance and the creation of the Arab state. Out of this marriage of convenience, Sharif Husayn ibn Ali (the emir of Mecca) denounced the Ottoman regime as an enemy of Islam and declared a revolt against it with himself and his family as the leaders of the future Arab state. Husayn claimed to represent all the Arab people and portrayed his action as a duty to Islam. Careful not to attack the caliph, he urged Muslims to rise up and liberate their caliph from the clutches of the CUP regime, whose secularist policies it depicted as violating the *Quran* and the *sharia*.

Britain promised to provide Husayn with supplies, weapons, and funds for his revolt against the Ottomans. In exchange for his commitment to an armed rebellion against the Ottomans, Husayn requested British recognition of an independent Arab state that would embrace the Arabian Peninsula and include the Ottoman provinces of greater Syria (including Lebanon and Palestine), and the provinces of Iraq—i.e., the Arabic-speaking world east of Egypt. But in the course of the war, the Anglo-French Sykes-Picot Agreement (1916), in contravention of portions of the British pledge to Sharif Husayn, divided the Arab-speaking Ottoman provinces in accordance with their own interests with little respect for the demands of the local population. This resulted in the splitting of Arab-speaking communities across different nations.[3] For example, Iraq was divided between Arabs and Kurds, and Transjordan was created by splitting the territory of the former Ottoman province of Palestine into Arab and Jewish sections.

Sharif Husayn emerged from the war as king of the Arabian region of Hijaz, a territory significantly smaller than he and his supporters hoped for. From the Arab perspective, the British pledges to Husayn had been sacrificed to the requirements of allied harmony and imperial self-interest. Among the Arabs, the year 1920 when Britain and France marched into the Middle East, became known as the *am-al-nakhbah*, "the Year of the Disaster."[4] Husayn's shortcomings, on the other hand, made him unpopular among the Muslims in the region, as he was blamed for the weakening and the eventual demise of the Ottoman Empire. Taking advantage of Husayn's political weakness, Abd al-Aziz ibn Sa'ud (1881–1953) in 1924 led his Wahhabi inspired Ikwan warriors into the provisional state of HIjaz, seized the holy cities of Mecca and Medina, and drove the *sharif* into exile. The new ruler of Arabia, the head of the house of Sa'ud claimed legitimacy based on the Wahhabi religious order that it helped establish.

Chapter 8

Islam and National Plurality

The Ottoman Empire was a conglomerate of linguistic, regional, and religious groupings, the balance among which was disturbed by European interventions, the ensuing political changes, and eventually the Ottoman defeat in the course of the First World War. In a series of post-war treaties, Britain and France carved up the former Arab provinces of the Ottoman Empire between them into protectorates and mandates. As a result, instead of one, several Arab states were created. At the beginning of the war, there were only a few Muslim states or state-like political entities. In addition to the Ottoman state, these also included Egypt, Morocco, Tunisia, Yemen and Iran. Less than ten years later, the political map of the region changed with the creation of the Ottoman successor states of Turkey, Iraq, Transjordan, Syria, Lebanon, and Saudi Arabia (in part). Of the ten core Middle Eastern states, however, only Turkey, Saudi Arabia, Yemen, and Iran exercised sovereignty. The Turkish model of radical secularism, with some variation, was replicated by Reza Khan (r. 1925–1941) in Iran, Amannulah (r. 1918–1928) in Afghanistan, and later Soekarno (r. 1945–1965) in Indonesia. All three regimes, much like Turkey, adopted this model in the absence of direct external (colonial) imposition.

In Egypt and the new states of Iraq, Syria, Transjordan and Lebanon, however, it was the British or the French administrators, with some support from local westernized elites, who created a system of constitutional secular states, expecting the new protectorates to develop legal, educational, political, and economic institutions. Nationalism as a foreign idea and a project of the state had a limited influence over

Muslim societies and was not a particularly useful tool in helping local rulers maintain a firm grip over society.[1] The new states would seek to impose strict central controls over rural and urban populations and to instill in all their citizens a measure of "national" uniformity. Secular legitimacy of political rule was provided in a series of postwar written constitutions (Egypt in 1923, Iraq in 1925, Transjordan in 1928, and Syria in 1929), in which foreign administrators specified the institutions and governing processes. The Iraqi constitution of 1925, for example, established a constitutional monarchy and vested the legislative power in an elected parliament. Parliamentary systems were also created in Syria, Egypt, and Lebanon.

Foreign administrators have also insisted that the Western (European) model of the separation of church and state be replicated in the protectorates. The Muslim states have been able to inject some Islamic provisions into their constitutions, such as the requirement that the head of state be a Muslim or that Islamic law be recognized as a source of law.[2] Similar to the Ottoman *Majelle* codification of the late nineteenth century, there were efforts to incorporate the *sharia* as a set of rules associated with Islamic tradition into a general legal system where they would coexist with Western legal rules. Most significantly, between 1936 and 1942, 'Abd al-Razzaq al-Sanhuri, produced comprehensive civil and criminal legal codes in Egypt that reflected both Islamic and Western values and the version of which would be adopted by other states.[3] Overall, the extent to which the Islamic legal tradition was integrated into modern legal systems of the protectorates varied both across countries and in accordance with the particular field of law in question. In criminal matters, most countries adopted the French or British systems of criminal justice; while in commercial matters, the majority generated a hybrid system, which combined French, Swiss, or British norms with various concepts and doctrines inspired by the Islamic legal tradition.

In general, only personal and family law remained mostly susceptible to Islamic influence. The protectorates typically treated the *sharia* as just another set of legal rules to be applied by judges appointed by the state. In the judicial system, the protectorates developed a hierarchy of state courts in which secular state officials replaced religious scholars as judges. It was the state judges who were given, by the constitution, the power to decide which cases should be referred to the religious courts and which belonged under the jurisdiction of the state courts. Once the *sharia* came to be seen as a set of codified rules, a judge without training in classical Islamic law could apply it. In sum, similar to the developments in the Turkish state, western-based legal systems increasingly replaced *sharia*, while western-educated secular professionals replaced the jurist experts in *sharia*.

By promoting modernity, the European administrators of the protectorates believed that they were assisting the local population. The Europeans embarked on social engineering and encouraged adaptations to secular Western culture believing that the only way to get the local population on a path of full self-governance was to have them adopt the Western practices. Some of the local elites shared that perspective. For example, prominent Egyptian writers of the interwar era downplayed Arab Islamic heritage by emphasizing the country's Greek and pharaonic past in an effort to connect it more closely with secular Western culture.[4] However, regardless of how noble the objectives of the European administrators may have been, the regimes in the protectorates were the products of foreign rule, which imposed monarchs recruited from non-native elites (e.g., Iraq) and other political solutions. By advancing the values believed to be superior, the Europeans created the sharp separation between the state and its people. Bedouin (tribally organized nomads), who in the pre-modern period constituted almost one-fifth of the population of the Middle East, were particularly resistant to strong central governmental control. Even settled urban dwellers were insulated from the weak states that presided over them by a far more dense and complex network of kinship connections than was the case in pre-modern Europe.[5]

By changing the role of the *sharia* and the nature of its application in the legal and judicial systems, the foreign rule marginalized the scholars much like the Turkish regime had done so. The new states paid homage to the *sharia* but were not Islamic in the sense in which the Ottoman Empire was. As in Turkey, the origin of legal norms governing day-to-day behavior was formally made to be not from the Islamic sources but from the administrative and legislative powers of the secular state.[6] By marginalizing the *sharia*, codification under colonial or quasi-colonial conditions in the 1920s and 1930s minimized the checks on executive authority that the scholars once enjoyed. In the absence of a genuine civil society, the installed rulers in Iraq, Syria, and Jordan obtained their legitimacy in an authoritarian manner, mostly by building states with a strong security apparatus.

Islam, however, remained important despite the ongoing process of secularization. In the public arena, acting as defenders of true Islam, the scholars openly challenged the state's secular policies especially with regard to the family law (e.g., Iraq).[7] As the institutional power of the scholars diminished, however, so did their political influence. The more educated, sober, and responsible element in Islam declined, leaving behind the underground religious groups. In the private arena, those underground groups would eventually politicize religion and utilize it as important source of political opposition to the unchecked authority of the secular state.

Chapter 9

Revolutionary Arab Regimes and the Continued State Building

Turkish racial nationalism of the 1920s became an important source of Arab nationalist thinking. The phrase "Arab world," implying the idea of a single people stretching from Morocco to Iran, was the creation of the small clubs of nationalists in Egypt, Syria, and Iraq in the last stages of the First World War.[1] That narrative of Pan-Arabism, rather than the one of individual Arab nationalisms such as Egyptian or Syrian, remained an important one throughout the interwar period. However, it was not until the end of the Second World War and the subsequent process of decolonization that this idea would be put into practice as a concrete policy. In a number of Arab states, the process of decolonization initially led to the military coups that sought to get rid of externally-imposed regimes. A series of regime changes in the 1950s and 1960s in Egypt, Libya, Syria, Sudan, Iraq, and Algeria (but not in Jordan) brought to power a new generation of military officers who abolished monarchies, declared republics, and promoted policies aimed at ending the political controls of the state by foreign capital. Initially, the new leaders (e.g., Free Officers in Egypt) were nationalists in the sense of claiming independence from foreign rule but with no predetermined views on specific political organization or ideological orientation of their states. Soon they adopted a secular state model and developed a socialist political agenda that included land reforms (i.e., the redistribution of farmland) and the broad-based nationalization of domestic and foreign-owned enterprises, banks, insurance companies, import agencies, and hotels.

The leadership change in a number of Arab core states during the 1950s had an important socioeconomic component to it. It consisted of a shift away from the members of the landed or professional elite (Egypt) and urban notable classes (Syria) to the sons of small peasant proprietors, minor government officials, and petty merchants, some of whom grew up on religious tradition.[2] Colonel Husni Za'im in Syria (1949), Lieutenant-Colonel Gamal Abdel Nasser in Egypt (1952), Brigadier Abd al-Karim Qasim in Iraq (1958), and other young military officers from the lower urban or rural strata of society sought to promote far-reaching social reforms that included the abolishment of civil titles (*pasha, bey*) and the extension of guarantees of the protection from discrimination on the grounds of race, sex, language, or religion. Land reforms (Egypt, Iraq) aimed at reducing the wealth and power of the landed elite and improving the living conditions of the peasants, while the large public sector turned the state into a principle entrepreneur responsible for capital formation and job creation. In Egypt, in particular, since 1962 the state guaranteed a government job to every university graduate.

In the first quarter of the twentieth century, the Egyptian nationalism centered mostly on political distinctiveness of the former Ottoman province and its native Arabic-speaking inhabitants. In the late 1920s, as the political opposition grew to the artificial nature of the imposed borders in the Arab-speaking lands, the idea of Pan-Arabism strengthened in Egypt as elsewhere in the region.[3] The 1948 creation of the state of Israel and the ensuing first Arab-Israeli war provided a further impetus for the strengthening of Pan-Arabism. Thus the 1956 constitution of Egypt described the country both as Arab and as a part of the Arab nation, implying the Egyptian regime's commitment to a cultural and political unity of the Arab-Muslim world. Soon afterwards in 1958, Egypt and Syria merged, albeit temporarily, by creating the United Arab Republic (UAR), hoping later to be joined by Jordan and Libya. Pan-Arabist proclamations and merger attempts continued until the 1970s. For example, the 1964 Iraqi constitution outlined Arab union as the ultimate goal of the Iraqi state; while in the 1970s, Syrian President Hafiz al-Assad made a bid for economic union with Iraq and Libya, and later attempted unsuccessfully to merge with Tunisia.

Arab socialism of the 1960s and 1970s was secular in its nature; much like the Turkish state it regarded Islam as a hindrance to developmental progress and modernization. Although in some instances (most notably in Egypt) the agents of regime change relied on Islamic groups for support and made promises to infuse Islamic values into the new legal and political systems state, the actual policies never matched the expectations of those groups.[4] Having attained political power, the ruling elites in most Arab states took over the administration of the *waqf* system. This policy, in large part, continued with the measures implemented by the centralizing Ottoman government in the nineteenth century, and was an effort to further break the hold of the *ulama* over *waqfs* and gain control of the revenues generated by the endowments. Syria and Egypt abolished the family *waqf* in 1949 and 1952 respectively. In 1953, Egypt nationalized the administration of the *waqf* system and in 1957 most of its properties, as part of its agrarian reform, with proceeds of sales designated for development projects. For similar reasons, Tunisia nationalized all of its *waqf* properties in 1961. As a side effect, the nationalization of the *waqf* system also deprived *sharia* schools of their principal source of financing.

Because of the social power of Islam and its ability to mobilize the masses, secular nationalist and Pan-Arabist states attempted to strictly regulate religion and then use it to lend support for their cause. Early on, Arab state leaders used Islamic doctrines selectively to legitimate their secular undertakings.[5] In Egypt, for example, Nasser quoted scripture when articulating his vision of Egypt's development; whereas the revolutionary National Liberation Front in Algeria depicted socialism as compatible with certain teachings of Islam. At the same time, the states made concerted efforts to assert their domination over religious institutions and bureaucratize religious scholars.[6] Egypt and Tunisia have gone farthest in establishing virtual domination in this regard. The Egyptian government managed to make the once prestigious Azhar University entirely dependent on government policies. Prominent government-appointed *ulama* were persuaded into issuing decrees and writing articles on the harmony between Islam and Arab socialism. In Tunisia, the regime turned the al-Zaitounah Islamic Seminary, effectively, into a university of comparative religion.

The post-colonial (independent) state continued the mission of the (British- or French-administered) colonial state to transform the societies over which it presided. It inherited significant autonomy from the colonial state, but it also augmented its powers in the process. Through its policies of land reform and nationalization, it weakened important rival centers of power such as landlords, business communities, and foreign oil companies. The very nature of the objectives of the socialist reform programs—the introduction of planned economies and new networks of social control—led the governments to expand the role of the state. Accordingly, the constitution-makers in individual Arab countries opted for political systems with strong executive power at the expense of legislative and judicial branches of government. Over time, this highly interventionist state has in large part distanced itself from the society it was supposed to serve. By seeking to penetrate the society deeply through the process of regulating the economic and cultural affairs of its citizens, the state steadily undermined traditional organization of society and eventually brought the issue of legitimacy to the fore.

Initially, the governments (e.g., Iraq, Egypt) were able to satisfy the large sector of the population by providing free public education and stable employment. At the same time, they limited access to political power to the ruling elites. In most cases, political parties were either non-existent or officially banned while the media have been brought under state control. Winning independence from foreign rule and the promises of Pan-Arabism and socialist change earned the regimes political capital for the first couple of decades of their existence. However, by the 1970s, the regimes had lost that credit and increasingly relied on political repression facilitated by a strong national army and the repressive apparatus of the state—the latter often financed by oil revenues or foreign assistance. From constitutional monarchies under foreign tutelage, most of the new Arab regimes developed into authoritarianism of one of the two kinds: a presidential system (Egypt, Syria, Iraq, and Tunisia) or military dictatorship (Libya, Algeria). Since state leaders often had limited legitimacy and ability to effectively control Islamic forces outside of state control, they invited Islam back into the public arena. Prior to getting into a discussion of the ways in which the variety of Arab regimes have done so and the consequences of these policy measures, it is necessary to discuss internal developments in one other key Muslim state during the period of state formation in the Middle East—namely the case of Iran.

Chapter 10

The Iranian State in the Early Twentieth Century

Modernization, in the sense discussed in the previous sections, reached Iran later than it did Egypt or the Ottoman Empire. Initially, the Iranian state played no direct role in introducing the *Tanzimat*-like reforms. The late advent of reformism in Iran was in large part a reflection of the significant role that the Qajar dynasty, in order to consolidate its dynastic rule in the late eighteenth century, conferred upon the *ulama*.[1] The Qajar's predecessors, the Safavids (1501–1794), maintained their legitimacy based on the claim that the head of their family, Isma'il, was the hereditary of the Safavia *Sufi* brotherhood and the direct descendent of the seventh imam. Isma'il himself claimed to be a divinely inspired early representative of the Hidden Twelfth Imam Mahdi.[2] As a result, in the Safavid dynasty the clergy was regarded as an integral part of the government. The Qajars (1794–1925), in contrast, could not claim the right to spiritual leadership comparable to the Safavids. What they claimed instead was the role of a protector of spiritual, financial, and political interests of the clergy from the challenges of a rival religious group, the followers of the messenger Baha'u'llah who emerged in the nineteenth century. By treating Baha'i as heretics and violently suppressing the spread of their influence in the Iranian state, the Qajars had established a bond with the clergy that was very different from the growing alienation of the *ulama* from the sources of temporal power in the Ottoman empire and other parts of the Muslim world (with the exception of Saudi Arabia).[3]

However, the role of the clergy in the affairs of the state during the late Safavid period and the rule of the Qajars has been strengthened independent of the temporal rulers by the outcome of the internal doctrinal debate within the Shiite clergy. One faction of the clergy, the *akhbaris* (passivist clergy), claimed that all of the knowledge of the faith had been contained in the fixed number of books that could be traced back to the earliest period of Islam, starting with the rule of the eleven imams and continuing through the sixteenth century when the Safavids established their rule. In the view of the *akhbaris*, the opinions of the clerics in the present time could not depart from those past writings; the job of the clergy, therefore, was simply to know what *akhbar* is. The competing, more present-oriented faction of the *usulis* (activist clergy) developed in the late seventeenth and early eighteenth centuries during the decline of the Safavid dynasty. Appalled by the arbitrary, immoral, and incompetent rulers of the period, the *usulis* claimed that the late Safavid shahs were leading the country away from the faith and openly challenged their right to rule the country. Given their perspective on the state of affairs at this historical period, the *usulis* saw themselves as having the primary voice in determining the direction society was going (because they knew what was good for society better than any other group in society). The clergy, they concluded, should intervene in current affairs and tell people what to believe.[4]

Unlike the *akhbaris*, therefore, the *usulis* claimed that the most learned scholars could, based on the individual intellectual mission (*ijtihad*), make new determinations on the faith. The idea that someone could exercise *ijtihad* on any major social issue, almost abandoned in the *Sunni* Islam by that time, started being emphasized in *Shia* Islam in the course of the nineteenth century. So in sharp contrast to *Sunni* Islam where the clergy had, in most cases, been co-opted by the state gradually, the *Shia* clergy claimed that those members of the religious establishment whose piety and depth of learning were deemed by their peers to be superior—the *mujtahids* as they came to be known—were empowered to render judgments on matters of law and religious practice. As exceptionally learned individuals, the *mujtahids* were uniquely qualified to exercise *ijtihad*. And the only people in a position to identify those, they claimed, were the clergy themselves, since the government simply had no competence of doing so. The *usulis* eventually prevailed in this doctrinal debate and the political effects of this outcome would become obvious in

1891 when Grand Ayatollah Mirza Shirazi, a *mujtahid*, successfully challenged the Qajar Shah for granting, for his own personal gain and at the expense of ordinary Iranians, a British citizen Major G. F. Talbot a control of the Iranian tobacco market. Shirazi's objection to the concession in the form of *fatwa* had two important effects: it was the first and successful demonstration of power of the *mujtahdids* (the clergy) vis-a-vis the state and gave the Grand Ayatollah an appeal of a populist leader upholding the rights of the merchants and of the poor against the encroachment of the shahs.[5]

So by the end of the nineteenth century, the *Shia* clergy asserted their right to select the *mujtahids* whose entitlement to *ijtihad* was now widely accepted. Moreover, after the Shirazi *fatwa* and the subsequent cancellation of the 1891 Talbot tobacco concession, the clergy demonstrated political power in defense of the interests of the commoners from the repression of the Qajar rulers and foreign economic intrusions. Lastly, the Iranian clergy, by keeping the ownership of land and other property and regularly receiving the *zakat* (the charitable donations), was able to maintain financial independence from the state. In contrast to progressive marginalization of the religious establishment in *Sunni* Islam, therefore, the clerics in the mostly *Shia* Iran maintained, if not elevated, their social prestige and political role. In contrast to the changing attitudes in Cairo and Istanbul, in Qajar Iran it was still considered a sign of greater prestige to be admitted to the ranks of the *ulama* than to become a member of the civil service.[6] Given the different paths of the nineteenth century political developments in Iran, on the one hand, and Egypt and the Ottoman Empire, on the other, the process of modernization and the building of the secular state in each of the two contexts would have markedly different political consequences.

Iran did not experience the governmental centralization that was such an important precondition for the transformation of Egypt and the Ottoman Empire. Also, European-inspired military reforms, which had been the original driving force behind the Ottoman and Egyptian transformations, were not carried out in Iran. As a result, the key actors involved in the Ottoman and Iranian constitutional movements, the former in the 1870s and the latter in the early 1900s, were markedly different. Whereas the Ottoman movement had been founded on a transformed bureaucratic elite and a reform-oriented officer corps, the Iranian movement, with no centralized bureaucracy, was led by a coalition of merchants, *ulama*, and European-oriented reformers.[7] In contrast to the secularizing *Tanzimat* reforms, the constitutional clauses of the 1908 Iranian constitution proclaimed that Islam was the official religion of the state. The constitution included a political compromise based on which the *ulama* did not promote their own vision of the Islamic state, which would vest sovereignty solely in God and would instead accept a constitution that extended sovereignty to people. At the same time, the *ulama,* in the Supplementary Fundamental Laws that had been adopted in 1907, saw that the constitution enshrined clerical supervision of the legislative process by constituting "a 'supreme committee' of *mujtahid* charged with scrutinizing all bills introduced into parliament to ensure that no law contradicted the *sharia.* Although conceding on the issue of sovereignty, the *ulama,* by institutionalizing its supervisory legislative, in fact perceived itself as effectively sharing legislative power with the government.

The different impact of the First World War on the Ottoman state and Iran was yet another reason for divergent paths of political development by the two in the 1920s. Whereas the Turkish state, emerging from the crumbled Empire, abolished the dynastic rule and established a republic, monarchy continued to exist in Iran. Institutional and social secularization in Iran under Reza Shah (1925–1941) had some important similarities with the Kemal Ataturk's reforms in Turkey both at the institutional and societal levels. For example, in 1928 the Iranian parliament (*Majlis*) adopted a new civil code modeled on that of France and the government established a hierarchy of state courts in which secular officials replaced the *ulama* as judges.[8] The state judges were given the power to decide which cases should be referred to the religious courts and which belonged under the jurisdiction of the state courts. At the societal level, secularization, again similar to the Turkish model, was regarded as a precondition for carrying out successful social change and development. This led to the mandate in 1928 that males were to dress in the European manner, and in 1935 that they were to wear a hat. At the same time, the religious schools were not abolished as they were in Turkey, and the Iranian religious establishment has never been placed under the state supervision as it had been in the Ataturk Turkey or the post-colonial Arab regimes.[9] Although the civil code retained aspects of *sharia* law in matters of personal status, many of its provisions, however, contravened the Supplementary Fundamental Laws and made the constitutional power-sharing provisions from the 1908 constitution dormant.

PART THREE
The Quest for Accountable State

Chapter 11

Pan-Islamism

In the last decades of the nineteenth century, the following three processes converged in the Ottoman Empire: First, the secularization of the legal and judicial systems stripped the state of the authority derived from God, and thus disrupted a pattern of Muslim rule that had existed from the time of the inception of Islam. Second, the emerging world of national identities undermined the political, economic, and cultural integrity of the Muslim community. Third, the diffusion of Western economic and cultural influence led to a sense of collective inferiority among the increasing number of segments of the Muslim population. As in the past, the response to a constraining set of circumstances in which Muslims found themselves came in the form of social and religious movements. One of the most articulate explanations of the sources of weakness in the Islamic world came from a Persian-born writer and political activist Jamal-al-Din al-Afghani (1839–1897). Al-Afghani focused mostly on the internal causes of the decline and argued that the apparent domination of the Christian West resulted not from its inherent superiority but from Islam's fall into a state of decadence and stagnation.[1] He criticized Muslim rulers for allowing European armies to invade their territories and permitting foreign merchants the control of their economies.

By allowing uncritical Westernization, the Muslims, according to Al-Afghani, appropriated values incompatible with their religion. The adoption of materialism, for example, undermined Muslims' faith in religion and deepened social differences; the separation of morality from legality eliminated the role of shame in maintaining social order; while the acceptance of secular sovereignty invited revolutionary change as the only mechanism for ensuring that the rulers follow the law. For Afghani, Islam played a fundamental role in fostering unity among the Muslims and was once a key to the greatness of Islamic civilization. It is therefore necessary to re-assert religious morality in public life, ensure political stability, and thus restore the cultural autonomy of the Muslim world.[2] Following Ibn Khaldūn, Al Afghani saw religion as a source of qualities, such as shame and trustworthiness that are essential for the common good. Religion, according to him, further provides a stable basis for solidarity ('asabīyah), superior to natural solidarity of the tribe or political cohesion of a nation state, and could thus become an effective source of order and stability. Most significantly, religion-generated solidarity could help Muslims mobilize for resistance. Despite racial and linguistic differences among Muslims, Islamic religion is a way of bringing the Muslim community together; it is a necessary source of unity, identity, and political mobilization.[3]

He thus called for Islamic solidarity and direct action against foreign encroachment that in his view would renew Muslims' sense of purpose. By claiming that Muslims' knowledge of their own religion was sufficient to provide answers to modernization, he rejected the need for Western legal codes and opposed the adoption of secular courts in Muslim countries. Instead, he called for the return of political authority, for a unifying political leadership modeled on the pious early caliphs, and a universal caliphate governed by the sharia. With respect to the nature of political rule in a thus conceived state, he saw no reason to replace monarchy with popular government. This is because he believed that the Muslims were not yet sufficiently disciplined to govern themselves well and still needed the tutelage of a ruler who would train them in the skills needed for self-government.[4]

Al-Afghani's Pan-Islamic activism eventually brought him to Istanbul where he came to the attention of the Ottoman ruler Sultan Abdul Hamid II (1876–1909). Al Afghani's claims concerning the importance of religion for social and political order and solidarity coincided with the Sultan's reaction against the wholesale adoption of Western-inspired Tanzimat reforms in the Ottoman Empire and his efforts to stress instead the Empire's Islamic heritage.[5] Abdul Hamid II used Islam as an instrument for increasing the influence of the state both internally, within the confines of the Empire, and externally to the rest of the Muslim world. Internally, he catered to the religious establishment, disadvantaged by the *Tanzimat* reforms, and downplayed Ottomanism and its proclaimed acceptance of the equality of all religions. Externally, he emphasized the Empire's "Islamic" character and reasserted his status as the caliph—the title that had been held in the political background for centuries—and called instead for Muslim unity behind the caliphate. To emphasize his role of a formal protector of the two holy cities of Mecca and Medina, the Sultan built a Hijaz railway that connected Syria on the east-Mediterranean coast with the west coast of Arabia.

Abdul Hamid's Pan-Islamism developed at the time of anti-colonial movements in a number of countries with large Muslim population (e.g., India, Indonesia, and Morocco). His revival of the idea of Islamic solidarity under the rule of a single caliph, drew further attention to the possibilities of casting off European domination through a renewal of Islamic solidarity. He could present himself (at least symbolically) as an alternative to French, British, and Dutch colonialism. However, the rise of the Young Turks in 1909, the decline of the Ottoman Empire, and the rise of Kemalism (all discussed in earlier sections) was a setback for Pan-Islamism. Pan-Islamic ideas would continue to be endorsed, for example, in the works of Mihammad Rashid Rida (1865–1935), a Syrian scholar, and Amir Shakib Arslan (1869–1946), the Lebanese Druze writer, but the movements' underlying notion of Islamic solidarity based on faith would be overridden by the creation of the system of secular nation-states.

Nevertheless, the revival of interest in Islam would not fade away entirely. The late nineteenth-century Pan-Islamic mobilization against colonialism eventually morphed into the *Salafiyyah* movement. First used by Al-Afghani's disciple Muhammad Abduh (1849–1905), the term *salaf* (the Arabic for ancestors) was associated with the contentions made first by al Afghani and Rida, and later by Muhammad al-Shawkani and Jalal al-San'ani that the study of the early Muslim community provided the surest guide to divinely approved behavior. This socio-political movement reflected a set of novel ideas that shaped ideologies and institutions of nineteenth-century Europe. It combined romanticist glorification of historical past and tradition and a teleological view of history viewed as progressing towards a more just social order. In this view, the function of interpretation could not be restricted by the existence of earlier interpretive commentaries (*tasfir*) and/or precedents in jurisprudence (*fiqh*).

According to *Salafists*, the history of Islam in effect stopped with the rightly guided caliphs and should resume after a fourteen-century interlude. Only the return to pristine Islam, to a largely mythical golden age of the Rashidun (rightly-guided) caliphs, they believed, would improve the overall condition of Muslim society and reassert moral virtues. Salafists were driven by the idea that Islamic values and ideals could be identified and applied without reliance on the scholars. By having a direct access to the Quran and the Sunna, individuals may interpret those on their own terms, even against the authority of the scholars. This increasingly accepted view among activists and reformers opened the way for innovative interpretations as long as they could be justified by analogy with decisions taken during the Prophet's time or that of his immediate successors. Salafists thus deconstructed traditional notions of established religious authority within Islam. In so doing they created opportunity structures for the twentieth century religion-driven movements led by non-scholarly activists.

Chapter 12

Proliferation of Religious Authorities

Since the 1453 Ottoman conquest of Constantinople (modern day Istanbul), a chief religious official (*shaykh al-Islam*) appointed for the Empire's soon-to-be capital also created the *de facto* official head of the religious establishment of the Empire as a whole. The *shaykh al-Islam* had served as a formal advisor to the Sultan on religious and legal affairs, as a chief appointer of officials in the state controlled seminaries, and as an ultimate person for judicial appeals originating from the court system. The abolition of the caliphate nearly five centuries later also ended the central office of *shaykh al-Islam*, a comprehensive religious authority in the Muslim world and allowed local religious authorities to gain greater significance. These new conditions marked a return to the historical period prior to the rise of the Ottoman Empire and the distancing from the notion that Islam should be administered under the central religious authority of the Muslim community as a whole.

By the twentieth century, in most *Sunni* Muslim countries of the Middle East, official Islam, represented by the individual officials appointed by the state, was increasingly seen as subservient to the colonial rule (the British or French mandatory authorities in the interwar period), the secular regimes (Turkey, after the First World War), or the revolutionary regimes (socialist, Pan-Arabist, following the Second World War). The scholars' limited jurisdiction, often reduced to the area of family law, made them seem marginal in influencing political issues and the affairs of the state. As a further blow to the prestige of the religious establishment, when the legal systems of individual states became Europeanized, the judicial function shifted away from the scholars to the people trained in Western legal codes. As a result, the *Sunni Muslim* scholars ceased to be a political constituency around which a political organization or a movement could be organized.

Since only a small number of *madrasas* survived as institutions of higher education, the number of individuals graduating from such schools gradually diminished. As the educational training for religious scholars declined, advanced knowledge of Islam was acquired privately rather than in religious schools. At the same time, the public educational system started producing a generation of literate Muslims, who would aspire to fill this apparent vacuum in religious authority. They responded to the demands of people to learn about Islam although they themselves often had no formal credentials to act as scholars and religious instructors. The spread of printing into the religious arena towards the end of the nineteenth century created a technological means by which the literate, whether qualified as scholars to write about Islam or not, could communicate with the diverse populations across the Muslim world. Initially, relatively low literacy rates limited the impact of this new medium. But as literacy rates dramatically increased through the expansion of the state school system, the audience grew larger too. Since the educational systems produced more graduates then the state bureaucracies could employ, the discrepancy created a new politicized class of the educated but unemployed. This new class, particularly susceptible to Islamic preaching, started joining the growing number of Muslim organizations affiliated with mosques.

In the earlier phases of Islamic history, religious institutions played a central role in the socialization of people from rural areas in urban settings. Although the methods of socialization varied across regions, the prevalent method was that of the institution of *waqf*, the trust that existed to provide resources to the mullahs and their religious activities. For a number of centuries, *waqf* had been a primary agency of socialization for people moving into the cities and adjusting to urban life. As *waqf* came under the jurisdiction of the state, starting with the second half of the nineteenth century—first in Egypt, then in the rest of the Ottoman Empire, and lastly in the Empire's successor states and Iran—the standard ways of providing social services in urban context, particularly in its core parts, began to fall apart. As a result, by the time of extraordinary increases in rural-urban migration (e.g., Cairo, Damascus, and Tehran) in the first half of the twentieth century, the process of socialization had not been functioning as before and the role of Muslim scholars in the socialization of populations originating from rural areas diminished.

As the role of official Islam waned, the vacuum was gradually filled by a number of Islamic organizations (e.g., *Sufi* brotherhoods) that were closely related to the mosque communities and focused on the distribution of social welfare services. Many of these organizations would emerge with their own sect leaders to whom the members of a local community would pledge allegiance. Smaller organizations that could present themselves as independent of the state, particularly in the cases in which the state was under the authority of colonial powers, became credible alternatives for the growing pool of people in need of social services. Such organizations soon gained significant credibility among the population; by the 1960s they were perceived as more effective in providing social services (e.g., health centers and dental clinics, water distribution, electricity, and garbage removal) than the state agencies, which were largely discredited by the allegations of corruption or a lack of connection with the common people. As the number of mosques increased, particularly in the Middle East, so did the number of communal associations around them. Moreover, such organizations would often have branches in more than a single Muslim country.[1]

Some Muslim organizations that belonged to this decentralized network of associations with different agendas and variable degrees of autonomy from the state were disengaged entirely from politics. For example, the India-based *Jamata-y-Tablir*, one of the largest such Muslim groups, with millions of followers in a number of countries around the world, seeks to reconcile the demands of contemporary life with the manners of the pious people who lived in the time of Muhammad by simply following the guidance of the Quran and the *Hadith*. Other organizations' objectives are primarily political and often the principle source of opposition. For example, *Hizb ut-Tahrir*, an organization that, like *Jamata-y-Tablir*, operates in a number of states around the world explicitly calls for the restoration of the caliphate. Typically, the political organizations that have emerged in the cities tend to differ from those in the countryside, particularly in terms of their objectives and social programs. Some of the rural groups that sought refuge in the mountains or deserts have a tendency to be more radical while the urban groups opted for political participation in the parliamentary process regardless of how restricted the latter may have been in individual countries.[2]

Chapter 13

Islamism

The collapse of the Islamic socio-political order and the system of values in the period after the First World War, led to a new generation of reformist thinkers and the birth of a new political program—Islamism. Much like Al-Afghani, Islamists diagnosed the failure of the Islamic society as a consequence of the abandonment of religion and made an appeal for religious and cultural authenticity. By calling for a return to an Islamic state, they sought to restore Islamic society to its rightful place in the world and make Islam relevant for the modern world. Islamists argued that the way to fight injustice in society was not through appeals for moral reform but through organized political activity. They not only rebelled against the state but also set for themselves a goal of transforming it. For the twentieth-century Islamists, as for the late-nineteenth century European labor movements, the modern state with its centralization of political power and surveillance became both the principal target and an instrument of a future transformation of society. Muslims were to pursue this goal by reconstructing Muslim political systems so that they look like Islam's first polity, the city-state of Medina where the government represented and gave effect to the Divine Will. Islamists thus demanded a fundamental reorientation of the organization and governance of all societies in which Muslims live. They advocated replacing existing political systems based on the "laws of men" with a system based, in theory, on the "laws of God."

Islamism developed as a modern ideology in competition with the two other domineering ideologies at the time—political liberalism and Marxism-Leninism. The ideal Islamic state, advocated by Islamist leading exponents, was usually limited to general principles without specifying a particular form of government. Since no blueprint exists for the modalities of an Islamic political system within the sacred texts, there is no consensus among Islamists over what kind of state would be desirable for Muslims. The Islamist conception of the state could therefore provide the basis for either a conservative or a liberal form of government. In either case, the implementation of an Islamic order did not mean a return to the form of government that existed in the time of the Prophet and his immediate successors; it was perceived as something suitable for the modern age.

Islamism was a new form of revivalism, one that was not driven, at least not in the *Sunni* Muslim communities, by trained religious scholars, but by lay political activists trained in arts and sciences. Islamists, following in the steps of Salafists, actually wanted to do away with the scholars' monopoly on the interpretation of the *sharia*, since they saw it as an obstacle to their objectives of a comprehensive transformation of the state. In the 1920s and 1930s, in the Middle East and South Asia, Islamist groups initiated a debate about the strategies necessary to reach this point. But as the discussion below will demonstrate, no single strategy emerged in those debates. Instead, a difference of circumstances in individual cases played a key role in shaping the thinking of individual Islamist thinkers, their specific political objectives, and the strategies of revolutionary change they advocated.

The Muslim Brotherhood, an organization founded in Egypt in 1928, typified early Islamism. Initially, the Brotherhood resembled an ordinary Islamic welfare society involved in activities such as small-scale social work among the poor, building and repairing mosques and establishing religious schools. Its founder and leader, Hasan al Banna, later shifted the organization's focus to social issues such as prostitution, alcohol, gambling, and inadequate religious education in schools. Al Banna criticized Egyptian society for accepting atheism, the pursuit of pleasure, and relentless profit seeking.[1] According to him, over the decades of uncritical adoption of values alien to Islam, Egyptian society had deviated from its true path. Only a return to a Muslim regime could prevent the society's further moral decay. In order to accomplish this objective, a tightly organized movement was needed to create a different kind of state through a tightly organized social movement.

His two-prong strategy comprised of the Islamization of society—teaching students how to implement an ethos of solidarity and altruism in their daily lives—and then the capturing of political power. Initially, Al-Banna's emphasis was on social evangelizing, instruction, and moral example. However, at its fifth conference in 1939, the Brotherhood defined itself as a "political organization." Two years later, at the follow-up conference, it made a decision to run candidates in national elections and contest seats in the legislature. The organization campaigned on religion-related issues such as the creation of an Islamic banking system based on interest-free loans, and also on the issues of the political left such as nationalization of industries, redistribution of land, regulation of the economy, and generous social welfare programs (e.g., unemployment benefits, public housing, and public health and literacy programs).

Al Banna's proclaimed long-term goal was a humanity united by the Muslim faith. But his immediate focus was on the transformation of Egyptian society. He had no clear definition of the sort of political system he wished for. Al-Banna's conception of the Islamic state in general terms included the following three requirements: the Quran as the fundamental constitution; a government that operates based on the concept of consultation (shura); and the executive ruler bound by the teaching of Islam and the will of people. As a pragmatist, he accepted Muhammad Abduh's premise that every society should be allowed to choose a suitable form of government based on its history and its present circumstances.[2] To al-Banna, representative governments, whether parliamentary or presidential, did not contravene sharia and he believed that the Brotherhood could take advantage of integration into the pluralistic system to further its goal of dawa, or religious outreach.[3] To him, working within the framework of the political system could be possible. Egypt's existing constitutional parliamentary framework could satisfy the political requirements of Islam for a Muslim state. But for some members, participation in elections was controversial because electoral institutions were closely associated with the West and Western political practice.[4] Disagreements and defections also followed over the allocation of funds, whether to establish alliances with individual established political forces in the country, and whether the use of violence to achieve political objectives would be acceptable or not.

In South Asia, an influential thinker, al Maududi, went further in developing the Islamist position. He blamed Muslim rulers of South Asia for abandoning pure Islam and for the decline of Islamic identity under the British rule in India. He took a term *jahiliyya*, which in the Quran refers specifically to the period of ignorance in Arabia prior to God's message to Prophet Muhammad, and gave it a new meaning. Rather than interpreting it as a historical period, he treated the concept as a "condition," a state of ignorance into which a society descends whenever it "deviates from the Islamic way."[5] He believed that the only rule under which Muslims could live freely and fully as Muslims would be one where Quranic provisions for personal and communal virtue would be implemented. Maududi claimed that sovereignty belongs only to God (*al-hakimiyya li'llah*), and that governments ought to represent and give effect to the Divine Will. God's sovereignty implies that such a state would be governed according to the path laid out by God for Muslims to follow the *sharia*. Unlike al-Bana's call for evangelizing, Maududi believed that religious values had to be asserted and that a process of change of the ethical basis of society requires conquering political power.

By using the European idea of the state as an enforcer of positive law, Maududi claimed that Islamists had to capture the existing state and then transform society by enforcing *sharia* by decree.[6] He believed in incremental change rather than in radical ruptures and rejected violence as a political tool. A revolutionary change, in his view, should begin at the top and permeate into the lower strata. The primary effort was to win over society's leaders, conquer the state, and Islamize the rest of the government.[7] In 1941, in order to put this plan into action, Maududi formed an organization *Jamaat-e-Islami* and set its goal as *hukumat-e-ilahiya* (Allah's Government or Islamic State). Although claiming to be for the creation of an Islamic state, his practical aim was to make the state of Pakistan Islamic by capturing political power and by enforcing the *sharia* within the boundaries of the state. Despite its Islamist activism and the claim that the political system in Pakistan that emerged after 1947 is un-Islamic, the party became committed to a constitutional political process in the 1950s.

Chapter 14

Islamism Radicalized

Islamism experienced a dramatic shift in Egypt in the 1960s. In conditions of political repression harsher than the ones faced by either al-Banna or Maududi, Sayeed Qutb turned Islamism into a militant strategy. In the circumstances of authoritarian rule of Gamal Abdal Nasser, Qutb saw Islam as having not only waned, as Hasan al-Banna claimed, but as having effectively disappeared from Egyptian society. Drawing from Maududi, he saw Nasser's regime in Egypt as a product of *jahiliyya*, that is, a rejection of Allah's sovereignty. As a result, Egypt had become a society where leaders had substituted the rule of man for the rule of God. Social equality, according to Qutb, is only possible under a divine sovereign, where each member is equal by virtue of common submission to God. Drawing from Ibn Taymiyya (1268–1328), he openly questioned obedience to a ruler who does not obey God. Since Nasser's tyrannical rule became the equivalent of rule by infidels, the tacit consent about the unquestionable obedience to the ruler was no longer valid. In order to restore dignity to Egyptian society, Qutb pronounced *takfir* (excommunication, the act of declaring another Muslim an apostate) against the Egyptian rulers and the political system over which they presided.[1]

Qutb's stated political objectives implied more radical strategies of revolutionary change. He rejected al-Banna's faith in the merits of instruction and moral example by working within the boundaries of the secular constitutional state. Working within the framework of the secular political system, according to Qutb, was not possible. The torturers and their regime, according to him, constituted the legitimate targets of armed rebellion. In order to find a way for legitimating an armed rebellion against the Egyptian authoritarian ruler, he invoked the notion of *jihad* against an infidel ruler. While the traditional concept of *jihad* concerned the relationship between Muslims and non-Muslims, Qutb's conception of *jihad*, under social and political conditions in Egyptian society, extended also to the relationships among Muslims (that is, among those individuals whom Qutb would distinguish as "true" Muslims versus "so-called" or "nominal" Muslims). An offensive *jihad*, according to Qutb, is the necessary response to an increasingly strident enemy. So for him *jihad* becomes the means of eradicating a *jahili* society in favor of an Islamic society that exercises sovereignty in God's name by applying the prescriptions of the Revelation.

Qutb held that the Islamic world's decline could be reversed only if a small group of "real" Muslims (*jalouia*) emulated the ways of the Prophet Muhammad and worked to replace the existing governments in Muslim lands with Islamic ones. In this view, the implementation of the *sharia* is not sufficient to qualify a government as Islamic; the head of state, or Commander of the Faithful, should be chosen according to Islamic precepts, and all institutions should be Islamic. This new Islamic state would have a government that would operate based on the Quranic principle of *shura* (consultation); it would be a collaborative effort between a ruler and the ruled. Since the *sharia* does not specify the form of such consultation, it leaves open the questions as to who will participate, when they will participate, and how they should participate. But regardless of the type of regime, the authority of government must be vastly circumscribed. Regulated by divine law, government would no longer be the source of legislation, but only of administration. In the instances where no guiding precedent could be found in divine law, the ruler acting on his discretion may pursue the welfare of the community as he sees fit. But even then, the letter and the spirit of the *sharia* would temper such broad powers. And because in this view the ruler's authority is entirely derivative, he has no claims to hereditary succession, special privileges, or elevated status.[2]

As other Islamists, Qutb shared the political objective of a state that would remake society according to the laws of Islam. However, when it comes to the strategies leading to the creation of such a state the differences among Islamists place them in two distinct groups. The first group believes in the original concept of *dawa* (preaching) as practiced by Hasan al-Banna and Maududi, as discussed above, as well as by the Muslim Brotherhood since the 1970s. The second calls for a violent takeover of the state as advocated by Qutb. Qutb's sentencing to death and his execution in 1966 made him a martyr (of *jihad*) throughout the Middle East.[3] In the 1970s and 1980s, some of Qutb's more militant followers took his ideas to their extreme conclusion by declaring the whole Egyptian society—not just its regime—to be in a state of *jahiliyya* and, therefore, a legitimate target of *jihad*. This *jihad*, similar to the one called for by Islamist terrorist networks elsewhere, not only aims at specific interests, actions, or policies, but it also rejects secular society and political institutions. It rejects Western civilization as such, not only for what it does but for what it is, as well as the principles and values that it practices and professes.

Chapter 15

Transnational Muslim Solidarity and the Birth of Global *Jihadism*

Al Banna's political activism has been limited to the state of Egypt. Maududi wrote openly against the creation of a Pakistani state, claiming that it would betray the interest of a large number of South Asian Muslims who would remain outside the new state, but accepted working within the boundaries of the new nation-state once it was created. Upon Independence in 1947, his *Jamaat-e-Islami* immediately reorganized along national lines into separate Hindi and Pakistani organizations. Qutb in his works addressed Egyptian society in particular and talked in terms of national-specific goals. Socio-revolutionary activism of all three thinkers that aimed at regime change was just one strain of thinking and Islamist activism that we could call "national Islamism." Another strain originated in Muslim solidarity of the late nineteenth-century Pan-Islamism (discussed previously) and the later attempts to restore the caliphate, first in the 1920s and then again in the 1950s. The Pan-Islamic movement that started in Egypt, Syria, and the other core areas of the Ottoman Empire swept across the Islamic world in the early decades of the twentieth century and influenced political developments in South and Southeast Asia perhaps more than in the Middle East. In British India, for example, the Pan-Islamic Khilafat movement (1919–1924) tried to influence the British government to protect the caliphate during the First World War and in its aftermath. The 1924 abolishment of the caliphate created a sense of enormous loss by Muslims in South Asia who felt that without it Islam had lost a crucial political center.

In the late 1950s and early 1960s, the increased salience of Islam reflected the regional political dynamics in the Middle East. In order to counterbalance the political influence of Nasser's secular (and socialist) Pan-Arabism, a movement that openly condemned the (conservative) Persian Gulf monarchies (Saudi Arabia, Kuwait)—the Saudi government asserted its global Islamic leadership as custodian of Islam's holiest sites (Mecca and Medina). By calling for "Muslim solidarity" (al-tadamun al-islami), it allied with other Muslim governments (e.g., Jordan and Lebanon) in opposition to Nasser and later his follower Qaddafi of Libya.[1] In 1962, Saudi Arabia entered into a military confrontation with Egypt in North Yemen and into a broader ideological confrontation with other (Syrian and Iraqi) radical Arab nationalism.[2] With the approval of the ulama, who had come to see Muslims of other countries as believers who should be supported both financially and politically, the Saudi government, embarked on a systematic campaign of promoting Wahab-bism to the rest of the Muslim world. In order to boost its religious credentials abroad, it created a number of state-funded organizations, such as the Muslim World League (Rabitat al-Alam al-Islami) in 1962 that distributed Wahhabi literature in all of the major languages of the world. In addition, it gave out awards and grants, and provided funding for a network of publishers, schools, clinics, mosques, organizations, and individuals. It trained and supported imams for mosques, distributed tens of millions of Saudi-approved translations of the Quran and religious literature. In addition, the Saudi government developed close ties with major Islamic movements such as the Muslim Brotherhood and the Jamaat-i-Islami.[3]

Muslim transnational solidarity was further strengthened by the Palestinian loss of Jerusalem to the Israeli forces following the 1967 war between Israel and the joint Arab forces of Egypt, Syria, and Jordan. This loss made the Palestinian issue central not just to Palestinians or Arabs but to the entire Muslim world and was turned into a transnational issue. The Saudi King Faisal established the "Popular Committee for Aiding Martyrs' Families, Prisoners, and Mujahidin of Palestine," providing support to the Palestinians. In 1972, it created the Organization of the Islamic Conferences (OIC) to provide coordinated support for, among other things, the Palestinian cause, and the struggle of all Muslim people in general.[4] Later in the 1970s, the OIC created the Islamic Development Bank to promote the development of an Islamic banking system and finance development projects in Muslim countries.

In Egypt and elsewhere in the Arab socialist countries (Egypt, Iraq, and Syria), the decline of Pan-Arabism and the 1967 debacle tarnished the reputations of the military regimes that had come to power in the 1950s. The failed programs of social reform and the unfulfilled promises of strength through Arab unity shattered hopes and dreams of many who believed that independence and the adoption of secular ideas would usher in prosperity. By that time, throughout the Muslim world a feeling developed that modernity was failing the Muslims, that the modern nation-states were not adequate political solutions for the needs of Muslims and that these Western models were not working.[5] This ideological void created an opportunity for an intellectual revival of Islam both transnationally and in specific national contexts. A rising consciousness of religion made Islamic symbolism more publicly visible.

In the next two decades, this cultural and ideological shift was further intensified by the impression that Muslims around the world had been under attack and systematically oppressed by outside forces. Numerous new conflicts developed that seemingly pitted Muslims against non-Muslims. Some of the most prominent examples included the Soviet invasion of Afghanistan (1979–1988), the Israeli invasion of Lebanon (1982), and the mass killings of Muslims in Bosnia and Herzegovina (1992–1995) and Chechnya (1992). In response to these events, a more alarmist and xenophobic form of Pan-Islamism emerged in the Muslim world, based on the view that all Muslims have a responsibility to help other Muslims in need.[6] As the international Islamic organizations sought to spread awareness of the plight of Muslims around the world, the perceived external threat led to a closer identification with Islam among the Muslims in general and gave new life to Pan-Islamism, an ideology based on the view that all Muslims were one people who had a responsibility to help each other in times of crisis.

Saudi funding to Islamic groups worldwide intensified dramatically after the 1979 Iranian revolution in order to counter the challenge from Iran's alternative revolutionary Islamic system. As part of their strategy to limit the potential spread of Iranian influence, Saudis funded the building of new mosques in Central and South Asia, North and East Africa, and Southeast Asia. Through the government-sponsored organizations, wealthy individuals and charities, the Saudis made sure that *Wahhabi* imams, teachers and textbooks would preach the style of Islam that, the Saudis insisted, was the only one true religion of Muslims, implicitly overriding other

Islamic traditions.7 Their conservative version of religion, flowed into *madrassas* around the world—as in Central Asia (Afghanistan), South Asia (Pakistan), or North Africa (Sudan)—where it combined with cultural and political circumstances and took on a life of its own over which the Saudi donors had little control. In sum, whether intended or not, the spread of *Wahhabism* ended up also promoting the growth of religious extremism in the Muslim world.

The *mujahideen* struggle against the Soviet occupation in the 1980s brought together Muslims from various corners of the world into a defensive *jihad*, as articulated by Abdallah Azzam, who actively recruited *mujahideen* fighters for the war effort against the Soviets. According to Azzam, this was a fight against a non-Muslim infringement of Muslim territory that qualified as defensive *jihad*, one that demanded the transnational involvement of all able Muslim men in defense of the given territory. In the 1990s, this conception of *jihad* was used to justify the involvement of *mujahideens* in Kosovo, Chechnya, and elsewhere. But the war in Afghanistan, by bringing together some of the veteran Islamists (from Egypt) and *mujahideens* also gave rise to offensive *jihad* aimed first at the Muslim regimes subservient to the interests of the West (e.g., Egypt, Jordan, and Saudi Arabia) and later in the 1990s directly to the interest of their Western supporters (e.g., the United States of America and the United Kingdom). While Azzam advocated defensive warfare within defined conflict zones against combatants in uniform, Osama Bin Ladin called (in the mid-1990s) for indiscriminate mass-casualty out-of-area attacks—a *jihad* global and permanent. Bin Ladin's Al-Qaeda, an organization created to carry out this offensive *jihad* recruited its members from the "salafi-jihadist" community—individuals who embrace an extreme puritanical form of *Sunni* Islam and the use of political violence.8

The success of the *mujahideen* fighters against the Soviet Union in Afghanistan brought Islam to the forefront for a number of Muslim fighters. After the Afghan war, some *mujahideen* fighters would continue to carry out defensive *jihad* in Bosnia, Herzegovina, Chechnya, and elsewhere where conflicts involved the Muslim population. Others went back to their home countries and joined the opposition to the authoritarian state. Islamism thus became "globalized" as a reformist and revolutionary movement both domestically and transnationally. Islamic ideology reemerged as a major force and became a reason for mobilization and political participation across the Muslim world. It has led to the creation of political parties, movements, and regional and global transnational networks. Various strains of Islamism developed, which are based on different national and regional contexts: some Islamist groups are parliamentary, others are extra-parliamentary; some are violent and others are not; some act against the government of the state, others aim at external adversaries; some are driven primarily by external forces, others by internal needs; some are against specific interests, actions, policies, or even countries, while others stand for a rejection of Western civilization as such, for what it is and the principles and values that it practices and professes. The latter include most prominently the transnational networks of Al-Qaeda and its affiliates in the Arabian Peninsula (AQAP), the Islamic Maghreb, and the Islamic State of Iraq as well as *Al Shabab* (Somalia), *Lashkar e Tayyiba's* (also in Paksitan), and the Salafi Group in the Land of the Two Rivers).

Islamist groups and organizations also often differ over a variety of foreign policy issues such as the type of response to U.S. policies in the Middle East and South Asia or the course of the Palestinian-Israeli conflict and/or peace process. This is also true with respect to the 2011 regime changes in the Arab world (e.g., Tunisia, Egypt, and Libya). For example, whereas *jihadi* ideologues generally supported the protesters, actual *jihadi* militant organizations were more confrontational (argued that success of a revolution is not determined by how autocrats are overthrown, but by whether the succeeding government imposes the *jihadists'* conception of Islamic law). Some Islamists argue in favor of theocratic conceptions of the Muslim polity and call for the restoration of the full classical Islamic legal system. Among those who call for the recreation of a caliphate (in its various forms) there are also significant differences. For example, *Lashkar-e-Tayyiba's* objective is the restoration of the *dawla Islamiyya* (Islamic state), but one that would not just recover Kashmir (like other Pakistan-based Islamist groups) but also recreate the Mughal Empire. Similarly, some *jihadists* in Indonesia talk of building a caliphate that would stretch across Southeast Asia.[9]

Chapter 16

Contemporary Majority-Muslim State and Islam

The danger of extremist organizations, both transnational and national, should not be underestimated and the influence they sometime exert over individual Islamist groups world over should certainly not be diregarded. However, given the spread of a variety of Islamist movements over the last three decades, extremist organizations are relatively marginal and not necessarily relevant for the specific political objectives of Islamist organizations and movements in individual countries. Islamist groups and organizations played an important role in the quest for independence of a number of Muslim-majority countries such as Indonesia in the 1940s, and Egypt and Algeria in the 1950s.[1] In Afghanistan, Islamic political movement started developing at the *Sharia* Faculty of Kabul University in the 1950s. Islamic parties such as the *Parti Islam Se-Malaysia* (Pan-Malaysian Islamic Party, PAS) and the Muslim Brotherhood in Syria have been involved in parliamentary politics since the late 1950s and early 1960s respectively. The so-called Sahwa (Awakening) movement grew on Saudi university campuses from the early 1970s onward under the influence of exiled teachers from the Egyptian and Syrian Muslim Brotherhood and have presented formal political demands to the Saudi governments in the early 1990s (the Letter of Demands in 1991 and the Memorandum of Advice in 1992).[2]

The Pan-Islamist movements of the late 1970s generated political pressure toward what might be described as greater symbolic Islamization. Islamist political activism made a long-term impact on the political dynamics of individual countries and prompted changes in the mode of governance and state institutions. So did a downturn in income from rent (oil and geostrategic partnerships during the cold war) in the 1980s. Social pressures that resulted from economic restructuring in the 1980s and 1990s compelled states to use Islam more systematically. Most Muslim-majority regimes faced the increasing pressures of the clerics or of various Islamist organizations. Generally, the regimes fell into one of the following two categories. The first category of states turned to Islam as defensive strategy to balance internal political forces and contend with the apparent lack of regime's legitimacy. For example, the governments of Egypt, Jordan, Tunisia, Turkey, Iran, and Indonesia all found it politically opportunistic to spur political participation or co-opt various Islamist movements and organizations in order to marginalize forces of political opposition (e.g., Marxist, radical Islamist, and liberal political groups). In contrast, the second category of states (e.g., Malaysia and Pakistan) used religion more aggressively as a way of establishing hegemony over society and of expanding the state's power and control.[3]

The success of either strategy varied widely across individual majority-Muslim states. Many of the incumbent regimes experienced difficulties in controlling the growth of influence of Islamist groups and introduced various restrictive measures to minimize it. Some were able to do so with administrative measures. For example, the electoral success of Islamists in Jordan in 1993 prompted the King Hussein regime to rewrite electoral laws and engage in gerrymandering, while the Soeharto regime in Indonesia, fearing challenges to its rule, restricted the access to the parliament to traditional Islamic organizations and barred the lay Islamist movement. Other regimes used coercive methods instead. For example, the Algerian regime resorted to the use of violence in order to block a likely success of Islamists in the run-off elections in 1991. Finally, the regimes in Iran (1979) and Sudan (1989), having failed to co-opt or crush the Islamist challenges, disintegrated and provided Islamists in each of the two countries direct access to power.

The following sections discuss the examples of four different countries to demonstrate a variety of strategies in dealing with Islamist challenges and their markedly different degree of success in so doing. The first section discusses the successful alterations in the Saudi mode of governance. The second looks at Egypt's mixed strategy of co-optation and suppression. The third section reviews the Pakistan's success in appropriating Islamism for the reasons of its national security. The last section discusses the failure of the Iranian monarchical regime to resist Islamic challenges and the nature of the revolutionary changes in Iran's state structures and policies that followed.

Islam as a Source of Legitimacy of the Saudi State

Since its creation in the 1920s, the Saudi state embraced *Wahhabi* Islam and derived its legitimacy from Islam's fundamental texts and tenets. The scholars have been actively involved in justifying Saudi rule in Islamic terms by issuing religious edicts endorsing the regime's specific policies that seemed at odds with the preferences of the conservative segments of the Saudi population. Some of the most significant policies included the invitation of foreigners to exploit oil (1932–33); the introduction of girls' education (1964) and of television into the kingdom (1965); and the stationing of American troops on Saudi territory (in the 1970s and again after the Iraqi invasion of Kuwait in 1990). The scholars also provided a formal approval of the abdication of King Saud and sanctioned King Faisal's taking over the Saudi throne (1964). Religious conservatives, particularly strong in the judiciary, could agitate against the Saudi royals and pose bureaucratic obstacles to royal decrees bringing changes. But in practice, the Saudi state is not one where power with the scholars is shared. It is rather a state that has bureaucratized the scholars and limited their ability to influence internal political affairs (subordinating the scholars and judges to the state).

Yet, the regime's claim to legitimacy based on Islam has made the ruling family subject to repeated questioning of its religious credibility. Reacting to the piecemeal and silent modernization of the Saudi society and increasingly visible materialism of the Saudi royals, enriched by dramatically increased revenues from oil in the 1970s, a band of religious radicals led by *Juhayman al-Utaybi* occupied the Grand Mosque in Mecca. The rebels never threatened the regime militarily and showed no aspiration to take over the government; however, by openly questioning the religious credibility of the ruling family, they threatened the regime's legitimacy. Having secured the approval of the senior scholars to use violence on holy ground, the Saudis attacked the mosque and silenced the rebels. A few months later, the Saudi government gave the scholars greater influence and poured unprecedented amounts of resources into Islamic institutions to ward off religiously inspired dissent. The Saudi government and charities spent hundreds of millions of dollars all over the world, endowing mosques, youth clubs, and Muslim schools that promoted *Wahhabi* teaching of Islam.

From the mid-1980s onwards, this Pan-Islamism came to play a particularly important role in Saudi political culture. In the 1960s, groups of the Saudi scholars, under the impact of the radicals from Egypt and Syria, progressively became politicized and began to challenge the House of Saud. The decline in oil prices in the mid-1980s emboldened the reformist Islamist Sahwa (the Awakening) movement and generated some political dissent in the Kingdom. To deflect domestic political criticism, the Saudi government promoted Pan-Islamism at home by praising the Afghan *jihad* in official media and providing support to Saudis who wanted to fight in Afghanistan. But in the early 1990s, after the first Persian Gulf War, when King Fahd allowed a large-scale deployment of U.S. troops on Saudi soil, the Sahwa movement took this as an opportunity to confront the regime by contesting its monopoly on Pan-Islamism as a source of political legitimacy. Sahwist clerics such as Salman al-Awda and Safar al-Hawali accused the regime of hypocrisy, saying it could not claim to be protecting the oppressed *umma* while at the same time allowing American soldiers to be stationed in the holy land. At the same time, the Pan-Islamist credentials of the Saudi state were challenged internationally by countries like Sudan and Iran, which stepped up their attempts to appear as the champions of the oppressed *umma*.[4]

Overall, however, the Saudi state has experienced relatively low intensity socio-revolutionary Islamism and very little violence directed against the regime compared to Egypt, Algeria, Syria, and some other Arab republics. Unlike the Front Islamique du Salut (FIS) in Algeria, the Saudi Sahwa movement never produced a significant violent offshoot. International political developments, such as the opening of the Guantánamo Bay facility in January 2002, the April 2002 battle of Jenin, and 2003 U.S. build-up to the Iraq War, produced new symbols of Muslim suffering and helped the global *jihadist* ideologues in the Kingdom. Despite the Al-Qaida on the Arabian Peninsula's (QAP) clandestine activities in 2003 and 2004 and the shootouts with the government forces, its campaign had little success. First, it lacked popular support. Influential Islamist opinion leaders such as Salman al-Awda, Safar al-Hawali, and Nasir al-Umar condemned the violence and urged the militants to surrender to the authorities. The Saudi regime, on the other hand, refrained from disproportionate reactions that, for example, characterized the actions of Algerian and Egyptian governments in the 1990s. Saudi authorities instead waged an effective battle for the hearts and minds of the population by portraying militants as revolutionaries who wanted to topple the government and kill innocent Muslims. By consistently labeling the militants as misguided rebels, and by using the media to highlight the Muslim casualties of the violence, the authorities were able to undercut the Pan-Islamic message of the QAP and rally the population against them.

In the Saudi Kingdom, traditional social structures have created a consensual political culture in which political dissent has been handled with cooptation more often than with coercion. These methods, at least in the Saudi case, turned out to be quite effective in containing political opposition without provoking violent reactions. The regime's oil wealth has facilitated plentiful resources for developing such methods. Some of the radical young *ulama* who have proved to be the outspoken critics of the regime, were imprisoned in the 1990s for opposing the regime's decision to invite American forces into the kingdom. However, after their release from prison in 1999, many of them seem to be reconciled to working with the regime and achieving their objectives through it. At the same time, King Abdulah has, since 2005, restored centralized power of the state by taking on the scholars and thus once again subordinating the scholars and judges to the state and undoing the bargain of 1979. He has called for sweeping reforms of the judiciary, the principle source of clerical power, by professionalizing the courts, standardizing the training of judges, and eliminating opportunities for judicial abuse. He has fired the country's highest-ranking judge, Saleh al-Luhaydan, who embarrassed the country when he declared it permissible to kill owners of television stations that air programs out of line with his narrow view of Islamic morality. He has further fired another prominent religious figure—the head of the country's feared Commission for the Promotion of Virtue and the Prevention of Vice, the religious police.

The pragmatism of the Saudi regime also extends to the foreign policy realm where the Saudi regime tries to shape the outcomes of actual and potential regime changes in North Africa and the Middle East. Although Saudi Arabia backed the Egyptian secular regime of Hosni Mubarak to his last days in February 2011, in post-revolutionary Egypt the kingdom was quick to closely connect to the country's new emerging political forces. As a result, the Saudis now exert influence with both the Muslim Brotherhood (which has never publicly denounced, like more radical Islamist groups do, the Saudi royal family's ties with the West) and the more radical Salafi group. Similarly in Yemen, the course of regime change, has been taken over by activists from the Islamist Congregation for Reform (Islah) the country's main Islamist party founded by leading members of the powerful, Saudi-backed Hashid tribal confederation, whose decision to turn against Saleh was a key moment in the uprising in this country.[5]

Islam as an Elusive Instrument of the Egyptian State

Islamist organizations in Egypt played a significant role in mobilizing against foreign rule and the creation of an independent Egyptian state in 1952. The successive governments of Gamal Abdel Nasser (1956–1970), Anwar el-Sadat, (1970–1981), and Hosni Mubarak (1981–2011) each initially sought to boost their legitimacy by engaging the Muslim Brotherhood and selectively allowing the Brotherhood and other Islamic groups to proceed with their social and political activities. As soon as such opportunistic policies of the regime provided openings for the Muslim Brotherhood to challenge the *status quo*, the regime would turn against the organization, either with administrative and legal measures or with brutal state repression. Going back to the 1952 military coup that ended the monarchy, the Muslim Brotherhood lent its support to the emerging regime of Free Officers. It did so with the expectations that the new regime would be responsive to the Brotherhood's demands to Islamize society. So when Egypt gained independence, the Free Officers, who have had close contact with the Brotherhood since the 1940s, regularly used the mosques to spread information about government policies. However, the new military regime soon showed no interest in sharing power or in tolerating political opposition and in 1953 abolished all political parties. While it could not immediately cut itself off from the political support of the Brotherhood, it denied the Islamist organization access to political power.

When in the following year the regime clashed with the Muslim Brotherhood's demonstrating youth activists, it accused the organization of an attempt to overthrow the government and pressed for its dissolution. The subsequent intra-governmental power struggle, involving General Muhammad Naguib and Colonel Gamal Abdel Nasser, put off a more resolute action on the part of the government. In the ensuing struggle, the Muslim Brotherhood sided with Nasser, who eventually emerged as the country's leader. Initially, Nasser allowed the Muslim Brotherhood to operate freely and placed some of the Brotherhood members in influential positions, granting them, among other concessions, control over Educational Ministry. In return, the Muslim Brotherhood publicly supported Nasser's policies.[6] But as the Free Officers failed to follow through with their promise to Islamize the new state constitution, this marriage of convenience was brought to an abrupt end. Following a failed assassination attempt on Nasser in 1954, allegedly by a rogue member of the Brotherhood, Nasser's behavior towards the organization changed completely as he brutally crushed the Muslim Brotherhood movement.

Nasser solidified his commitment to building a secular Egypt with his policies regarding Al-Azhar, a leading religious and educational institution with deep involvement in the cultural spheres, and a very influential committee for issuing fatwas. In 1961, he brought this prestigious religious university under the authority of the state and added a wide range of secular degrees to the university's curriculum, including those in business, economics, science, pharmacy, medicine, engineering, and agriculture. In line with his policies of gender equality, an Islamic women's faculty was also added that same year. Nasser and his successors worked to control the institution by designating the Sheikh al-Azhar more on political than on purely religious qualifications. In an attempt to marginalize the Islamists, Nasser established a newspaper Minbar al-Islam that provided a mouthpiece for the Islamic justification of the government's policies.

The pattern of initial co-optation and subsequent repression of the Brotherhood continued during Anwar el-Sadat's rule. In order to consolidate his power in the early stages of his administration, Sadat moved away from Nasser's Pan-Arabist nationalist rhetoric and publicly endorsed Islamic values.[7] He had the educational curriculum re-written along religious lines and amended Article 2 of Egypt's constitution to stipulate that sharia was the "main source" of the nation's laws.[8] In 1971, the government closed down the concentration camps for political prisoners and by 1975 completed the release of the imprisoned Brotherhood members. He removed government restrictions on the Muslim Brotherhood's core activities in Egyptian society and allowed the organization to operate as a semi-legal network and even publish its own magazines and a monthly newspaper, *Al-Da'wa* ("The Invitation to Islam"), whose circulation reached 100,000 by the early 1980s.

These government policies created the new opportunity structures that allowed Muslim Brotherhood to expand rapidly into university campuses, labor unions, and professional syndicates.[9] But the government stopped short of approving the Brotherhood's quest for permission to operate legally and to organize itself as a political party whose representatives would stand for office in parliament. Instead, in 1977, the Egyptian legislature passed the Political Parties Law that specifically prohibited the formation of parties based on religious affiliation. The government's restrictions on the Brotherhood's political participation was only one of the reasons for the increasingly sour relationship between the organization and the regime. Over the years of Sadat's rule, the Muslim Brotherhood and its more radical offshoots came to deplore what they perceived as progressive Westernization of the country, corruption of the Egyptian public life, and increasingly conciliatory policies towards Israel. Sadat's signing of the separate peace treaty with Israel in 1979 and the coming to power of Islamist fundamentalists in Iran that same year served to radicalize educated but unemployed urban youths. In response to growing violence between Christians and Muslims, in September 1981, only weeks before his assassination, Sadat turned to repressive methods of the state and arrested hundreds of politicians of all stripes, including scores of Muslim Brotherhood members.

The Mubarak regime initially repeated Sadat's attempt to provide limited public space to the Brotherhood. Although the organization remained officially illegal and was not allowed to distribute literature or assemble in public, the state tolerated the publishing of the Brotherhood's two newspapers (*Liwa' al-islam*, "The Banner of Islam," and *al-I'tisam*, "Adherence"). The Mubarak regime also allowed it to maintain regional and national offices, make public statements, and field its candidates as independents or as members of other parties in local and national elections. Whereas the state heavily pressured radical Islamist groups, it gave moderate Muslim Brotherhood members the opportunity to participate in formal political institutions. With this new political opening, the Muslim Brotherhood established political presence in both parliament and professional organizations and emerged as the primary opposition to the ruling National Democratic Party.[10] In the 1984 elections, the Brotherhood members were allowed to run candidates for the Wafd party and in 1987 for the Labor Party, with considerable electoral success. Similarly in the 1989 elections, the Muslim Brotherhood won a plurality of the vote and in 1991 gained control of five ministries, including education, health, justice, religious affairs, and social development, as part of a short-lived coalition government.

The Brotherhood's electoral success and the spread of its network of social services (filling in for the state) clearly indicated the organization's growing influence in the first decade of Mubarak's rule. This trend continued in the early 1990s and coincided with the increased violence of extremist Islamist groups during the first half of the 1990s. But as the confrontation between the regime and more radical Islamist organizations (al-Gama'a al-Islamiya) intensified, the regime conflated the two trends and once again suppressed Muslim Brotherhood's activities with a heavy hand.[11] So in 1993 professional associations were placed under direct state control and in early 1995 over a thousand Brothers were arrested.[12] A failed assassination attempt against Mubarak in Ethiopia later that same year further exacerbated Islamist-regime tension.[13]

As the regime's relations with the Brotherhood improved yet again after 1997, the Islamist organization continued with its social and political activism, although under significant state-imposed constraints. For example, in 2000 the Brotherhood gained seventeen parliamentary seats despite the government's strenuous media campaign against it and the arrests of several of its candidates shortly before the vote. A year later, it gained all the seats it contested in the Lawyers' Association open elections for its executive board. Mubarak responded through a constitutional amendment prohibiting political parties based on religion. Nevertheless, in the 2004 parliamentary elections, members of the Muslim Brotherhood ran independently and won a considerable number of seats (88 seats or 20 percent of the total) to form the largest opposition bloc, despite numerous violations of the electoral process and the arrests of hundreds of Brotherhood members who were tortured and held without being tried for prolonged periods of time. The Brotherhood also began participating in pro-democracy demonstrations with the Egyptian Movement for Change (Kifaya, "enough"). Once again in 2007, the Mubarak regime responded by amending the state constitution to ban independents from running for offices, which effectively disabled the Brotherhood from contesting parliamentary elections. In 2008, the state disqualified most Brotherhood candidates in the local council elections and again launched a wave of arrests and military trials against the organization's members. Towards the end of Mobarak's rule in 2011, the regime, in order to further undermine the Brotherhood's influence, also allowed a growth of influence of a conservative Salafi group whose followers observe the purist rules of Islam's early days.

The State Appropriation of Islam: The Case of Pakistan

The founders of the Pakistani state regarded Islam as an instrument of integrating the country's diverse ethnic groups (e.g., Bengalis, Balochs, and Pashtuns) and provinces (e.g., Kashmir and the North West Frontier Province), but sought the state based on popular sovereignty and the separation of powers. Despite the pressures of the Islamists—most notably of the *Jamaat-e-Islami* (JI)—to create an Islamic state ruled by the *sharia*, similar to the developments in Egypt after the 1952 revolution there, the secular nationalist view prevailed. Nevertheless, the *Jamaat* influenced the constitution-writing process between 1949 and 1956 and remained active until finally being marginalized in the 1958 military coup. The coup, in part, reflected the fact that the constitution of the new state failed to settle the critical issues such as the division of power among various branches of government, the jurisdiction of the country's provinces, and the role of religion in matters of state.

The return to civilian rule in 1971 provided another opportunity for the Islamists to influence the social and political agenda and extract concessions from the Zulfiqar Ali Bhutto government (1972–1977). Specifically, the 1973 constitution formally proclaimed Islam the state religion and created the Islamic Advisory Council to recommend ways and means to bring existing laws of the country in conformity with the Islamic principles. It instituted the judicial review of legislative actions to guarantee that they do not violate Islamic law or values (a so-called "repugnancy clause," mandating that a judicial body overturn laws repugnant to Islam). As a further concession to the *Jamaat* and other Islamic groups, the government also banned alcohol consumption. The Bhutto government, however, tried to control the influence of Islamists by founding a newspaper called *Musawat* as a mouthpiece for the Islamic justification of the ruling party's policies. It also pressed forward with the expanded role of women in the public arena over Islamist objections. Another military coup in 1977 that abruptly ended the Bhutto rule provided, perhaps somewhat unexpectedly, an opportunity for the Islamists to assert their political agenda even more aggressively.

In order to reduce ethnic pulls in the state, the Zia-ul-Haq military regime (1977–1988) made Islam central to the Pakistani national identity. It took measures, similar to the one by the civilian Malaysian government a few years earlier, to Islamize political, legal, and economic structures of the state. From the 1980s onward, the state took control over religious education, jurisprudence, taxation, and social services.[14] The regime opened the government to the *Jamaat's* influence to an unprecedented extent as the *Jamaat* began to infiltrate into the armed forces, the bureaucracy, important national research, and educational institutions. The government established a *Sharia* Council, composed of religious scholars, with an oversight of the constitutional and legal matters of the state and a consultative body to the president, the *Majlis-i-Shoora*, composed of religious scholars and devout Muslim professionals as a body to replace the National Assembly. In the economic sphere, the government created a "profit and loss sharing system" according to which an account holder would share the bank's losses and profits. It allowed the number of mosques to increase and encouraged the establishment of *madrassas* as an alternative to public schools. The *Jamaat* and other Islamists also became major beneficiaries of the 1980s Afghan insurgency against the Soviet Union, which was launched with massive assistance from the United States and Saudi Arabia and micromanaged by the Pakistani regime. By promoting Islamization in society, the regime was able to subdue political opposition and expand its power and capacity without much resistance.

Yet, radical Islamization of the country did not have much popular support in Pakistan at the time. Faced with the countrywide protests in 1979, the Zia regime stopped short of implementing *sharia* laws in 1979. Political opposition, for the most part, saw Islam as a principal component of the legitimacy formula to fend off demands for a return to democracy. The regime's calibrated Islamization, on the other hand, antagonized the Islamists. The increasingly militant *Jamaat's* student (and more radical) wing, the *Jamiat-i-Tulaba-i-Islam* (the Islamic Society of Students) regularly clashed with other student groups on Pakistani campuses. When the government eventually banned student unions in 1984 and brutally repressed remnants of the resistance of *Jamiat-i-Tulaba*, it inevitably alienated the Islamists. The *Jamaat* became increasingly disenchanted with the regime as it became apparent that the military regime had in good measure dissipated Islam's political appeal and diminished the ability of religion to legitimate political action and authority.

Since the Pakistan's return to civilian rule, following the Soviet withdrawal from Afghanistan in early 1989, the Islamists, including the *Jamaat*, continued with their political activism and participation in the parliamentary elections. Although well-financed, the Islamists were not able to obtain much support from the Pakistani electorate in the 1990 and 1993 elections prior to yet another military coup in 1999. Their major political victories since have been won in large part as a result of the military regime's concessions in return for garnering political legitimacy and achieving strategic objectives. The Islamists' only strong showing in the 2002 elections (11 percent of the popular vote and 20 percent of the seats in the lower house of parliament) did not indicate a significant shift in public attitudes toward Islamists. Rather, it resulted from the fact that Pervez Musharaf's military government prevented two former ministers, Nawaz Sharif and Benazir Bhutto from participating in the election. In contrast, the candidates of the alliance of Islamic parties—the *Mutahhida Majlis Amal* (United Action Council)—did not face disqualification, and Islamic party leaders campaigned freely, which explains their electoral support that year.

The *Jamaat* and other Islamist parties continued to have close relations with the Pakistani military and its Inter-Services Intelligence (ISI) agency. Since the late 1970s, the military and the ISI have trained and directed thousands of militants to fight in Indian Kashmir, an area that Pakistan has claimed since independence in 1947, and in Afghanistan, the control of which it considers crucial for its national security. Despite the efforts of the civilian government of Nawaz Sharif in 1999 to dismantle radical Islamic groups, the Pakistani military, unaccountable to parliament or the courts, has continued to use Islamists for political purposes both domestically and across the Pakistani borders. So the military continues its support for the Taliban in Afghanistan and *Jaysh-e-Mohammad* (JeM), and *Lashkar-e-Tayiba* (LeT) in Kashmir. Years of religious rhetoric have influenced a younger generation of military officers. As a result, a number of ISI officials have assimilated the Islamist beliefs they were rhetorically called on to support in the course of *jihad* in Kashmir and Afghanistan in the 1980s.[15] But the use of Islamic extremists to pursue foreign policy goals and agendas for several decades in India and Afghanistan has now backfired as it has created in the Pakistani tribal area an internal extremist movement *Tehrik-i-Taliban Pakistan* (the Pakistani Taliban). Since 2008, Tehirk has targeted the armed forces and civilians and in 2009 expanded its activities outside the tribal regions to the Swat and Buner districts in the western part of the country, provoking a major counteroffensive by the Pakistani army.

Prior to 2001, among the Islamist groups represented in the Pakistani parliament, the *Jamaat* traditionally enjoyed the most popular support. The Pakistani government's decision in late 2001 to join the United States in its war against the overwhelmingly Pashtun Taliban network has led to a shift of electoral support away from the lay Islamists of the *Jamaat* and to the *Jamiaat-e Ulema-e Pakistan* (JUI), a party of mainstream Islamic scholars who abandoned their traditionally quietest stance in politics and took a more activist role. The JUI, led by puritanical Deobandi *ulama* has a strong political base among the Pashtuns living in the North-West Frontier Province (NWFP) and Baluchistan. This shift that began in the 1980s manifested itself clearly in the October 2002 elections when the JUI, campaigning in electoral coalition with the *Jamaat*, won more votes than its well established partners, showing that the combination of Pashtun nationalism and traditionalist Islam (rather than the lay Islamism of the *Jamaat* variety) seemed to have the greatest political appeal in Pakistan. Significantly, in 2008, the *Jamiaat-e Ulema-e Pakistan*, distinguished itself from the *Jamaat-e Islami* by condemning the actions of *Tehrik-i-Taliban Pakistan* against the government and lending its support to military operations in Swat.

Iran: The Islamic State

By the 1960s, the Iranian clerical establishment was increasingly disturbed by the policies and political reforms pursued by the Reza Pahlavi regime (1941–1979). Particularly, the shah's policies of land reform, which abolished the feudal land system, threatened to dispose the leading *ulama* of the vast resources they controlled and thus undermine their financial autonomy. The Pahlavi regime's close foreign relations with Israel and the regime's ostensible deference to the United States further alienated the clerics. As the regime repeatedly failed to redress public grievances and responded instead with repression, the clerical-led political opposition became increasingly radical. Acknowledging this, the government made an effort to co-opt parts of the clerical establishment by creating a Religious Corps. This body, which was to recruit from graduates of the theology departments of state universities, was to effectively create the government's mullahs. But this new religious body never became large enough to make a greater political impact. Although the Pahlavi government wanted high religious leaders resident in Iran to speak against the rebellious mullahs, they refused to comply. Instead they increasingly worked to oppose the regime.[16]

The earlier section on Iran established that by the beginning of the twentieth century the more activist faction of the *Shia* clergy—the *usulis*—prevailed in the doctrinal debates over the practice of *ijtihad*. But even within this activist school, there had been no consensus on the issue of whether the clerical power should be confined to ethical and legal issues or extend to the public policies and the governance of the state. Until the 1960s, the leading *ulama* expressed their distrust of secular power more in terms of detachment from the political arena (political quietism) than in terms of direct engagement in political matters or active opposition to the existing regime. This policy changed dramatically in a series of events in the next two decades, culminating with the 1979 toppling of the Pahlavi regime.

The passing of Grand Ayatollah and *marja-i taqlid* (the source of imitation) Seyyed Hossein Tabatabai Borujerdi in 1961 provided an opening for the overt questioning of further political quietism on the part of the *Shia* clerics. Amidst the uncertainty over Borujerdi's immediate successor, Grand Ayatollah Ruhollah Khomeini publicly voiced his opposition to the Pahlavi rule and soon encouraged others to join him. He initially accused the shah of being opposed to Islam, to the existence of the religious class, and to the constitutional clauses that frame the state in Islamic terms. Furthermore, he threatened the shah's rule by saying that if the ruler of Iran did not act as a Muslim he would be expelled. Finally, Khomeini denounced the shah and called for the end of the monarchy. In a series of lectures in 1970, he argued that the institution of monarchy was "unIslamic." By insisting that God had sent Islam to be implemented and had commanded an Islamic type of government, Khomeini called for a political rule in which the holders of various state offices would have knowledge of *sharia* and the state in which Islamic rather than secular courts would administer justice. Khomeini's reasoning was the following: since no one knew religion better than the *ulama*, the religious scholars had to rule if God's command was to be executed. The state's ruler, according to Khomeini, should therefore be a jurist (*faqih*) expert in Islamic law and justice with governing skills.

Khomeini clearly regarded Islam not only as a source of rules for acts of worship and morality but also as a source of regulating social and political affairs. A learned leader, in this view, would not only be involved in guarding laws and voicing opinions but also in controlling the application and enforcement of laws, that is, in governing the affairs of the state. Khomeini articulated this idea by saying that until the return of the twelfth imam a divinely anointed senior cleric should rule in his stead. In order to provide further justification for his claim he invoked the nineteenth-century concept of *wilayat al-faqih* ("guardianship of the jurist"). The scope of guardianship implied by this concept has been debated widely among the *Shia* clergy ever since the late 1800s and ranges from issues such as custodianship of endowments to the governing of state institutions. Khomeini's was thus a maximalist interpretation (absolute *wilayat al-faqih*) of the term. By eclipsing the more moderate visions of guardianship, he succeeded in combining the role of Shiite theologian with that of political leader of the (global) Muslim community.

Khomeini's concept of Islamic government, however, lacked clarity. He anticipated, in most general terms, that the clerical classes would lead the Islamic state and that the political community would be modeled on the Prophet's city-state of Medina. He assigned to the government the traditional duties of protecting Islam, defending the frontiers, administering justice, and collecting taxes. But he grappled with the questions of what institutions to include in such an Islamic state. Instead, the nature of the state institutions would be decided in the course of the constitutional debate following the 1979 revolution. While the coalition of forces that toppled the Pahlavi regime agreed on the abolition of monarchy as its principal political objective, it lacked both unity and clarity about the constitutional nature of the state, the composition of the new government, and its policies.[17]

There were conflicting opinions regarding issues such as the nature of political authority, the role of popular sovereignty, individual rights, and judicial independence in the state. Many called for the principle agents of the revolutionary change (the clerics) to be made accountable to the public and the instruments of their political influence (the Revolutionary Guard and revolutionary courts and committees) to be merged with the regular institutions of the new Republic. Even the Islamic groups called for the accountability of political power. For example, the Islamic People's Republican Party (IPRP), founded by a group of bazaar merchants, middle-class politicians, and clerics associated with Khomeini's chief rival in Qom, Ayatollah Shariatmadari, emphasized collective religious leadership and criticized the unruly behavior of the revolutionary committees and the harsh judgments of the revolutionary courts

Not all of the forces involved in the constitutional debate had equal opportunity to have their voices heard by large segments of the Iranian population. This explains why the Iranian Revolutionary Party (IRP) that controlled a large network of mosques and clerics across the country, most of the security apparatus, and the broadcast media was able to eventually overwhelm its political opponents. The IRP and most other Islamic parties sought to enshrine Islam as the basis of the constitution, of the institutions of the state, of its economic and judicial system, and even of the institution of the family (by rejecting the idea of equality of men and women). They insisted that the president and prime minister be practicing *Shia*, knowledgeable in Islamic law, and that a religious test be applied to the commanders of the army.

The IRP and other Islamic parties desired to give a right of veto over all laws to the Council of Guardians, empower the Islamic jurists to appoint judges, supervise the judiciary, and approve presidential candidates. They also injected into the debate over the constitution the concept of government by the Islamic jurist (*faqih*) and set aside the criticisms by some that to establish a government avowedly *Shia* in character before the return of the twelfth Imam would amount to sacrilege. Over time, the pressures of the IRP and other Islamic parties successfully moved the discussion away from public accountability of office holders in the state institutions and closer to religious tests for leading positions with no need for consent of the faithful.

In the early phase of the constitutional debate, Khomeini refused a free choice on the form of government that would replace the monarchy and insisted on an Islamic state; however, he was not opposed, in principle at least, to a broad-based constitutional debate. Claiming his fear of the pressure from non-Islamic groups as the debate unfolded, he did little to change the direction of the increasingly skewed constitutional debate. The resulting constitution eventually created a state with a significant concentration of power. It made the *faqih* the central figure in the political order, enshrined the dominance of the clerics over the state institutions, entrenched Islamic jurisprudence as the foundation for the country's laws and legal system, and limited individual freedoms to what was considered permissible under Islam. Formally or not, the executive, legislative, and judicial branches of the government have all been subsumed under the absolute sovereignty of the supreme leader. The constitution further provided for a twelve-man Council of Guardians empowered to veto all legislation in violation of Islamic or constitutional principles and reserved to the six Islamic jurists on the council the power to declare laws in conflict with Islam. The clerics rejected the idea of equality of men and women and noted specifically that under Islam women could not serve as judges or governors.

A clerical monopoly of power in Iran thus resulted from a relatively long and not entirely intended political process by most political actors involved. The Iranian state eventually evolved into one where Islamic system of governance granted the sovereignty to God and through him to the Prophet, the imams, and the jurists. It developed into a theocracy that drew its legitimacy from the charisma of the revolution's principal leader. Not all of the senior *Shia mujtahids* in and out of Iran had given support to Khomeini's principle of rule by Islamic jurist and the vision of an all-powerful supreme leader. The absolute authority that Iran has extended to the supreme leader has been a subject of numerous criticisms by other *Shia* theologians. For example, Lebanese scholar Chibli Mallat argued that it went against the traditional system of choosing a leader in *Shiite* society where the leader emerged historically through an elaborate process of peer recognition. To a number of other theologians, the authority of supreme leader neglected popular sovereignty, which they see as compatible with a more democratic system of governance.[18] Some have also discussed alternative models of Islamic governance. Most notably, Baqir Sadr, who prior to being executed by Saddam Hussein's regime in 1980, had proposed a more democratic form of Islamic governance that would require the consent of the faithful and a consensus among *Shiite* clerics in choosing the preeminent religious leader.[19]

Further alienation of the allegedly Islamic state from the faithful resulted from the succession of power that followed Khomeini's death in 1989. The constitutional referendum that was to confirm Khamenei's legitimate succession as the Supreme

Leader eliminated the requirement of the *marja* religious status for this preeminent position in the country. The new Supreme Leader's lack of religious credentials made the clerical system's legitimacy based less on the charismatic authority of the ruler and more on the militarization of political power. On the other hand, the increasingly apparent lack of sufficient experience and technical expertise of religious leaders made them seek further centralization of power and become increasingly dependent on coercion. For example, besides being the head of state, the commander in chief, and the top ideologue, Khamenei also exercises significant control over the *Majlis* (Parliament) and the judiciary branch (including media censorship), both allegedly for the protection of national security. In contrast to Khomeini, Khamenei has empowered the Revolutionary Guards politically and economically and has given them control over the *Basij*, an all-volunteer paramilitary organization to help with law enforcement, the policing of moral issues, and the provision of social services. The powers of the Council of Guardians have also been extended to include filtering out all candidates for the presidency, the *Majlis*, and the Assembly of Experts (a clerical body that, in turn, elects and supervises the supreme leader).[20]

Ironically, the Iranian revolution that sought to end the shah's authoritarianism resulted in a regime seemingly not less repressive. Iran's government claims to rule with a divine mandate. Accordingly, what constitutes the law in the state is essentially defined not by popular vote but by what the *ulama*, or council of religious teachers, sanctions. Since the state thus takes a doctrinal position of religion, it inevitably becomes oppressive to those who do not agree with the doctrine as it seeks their conformity to it.[21] Moreover, as religion gets attached to political power it becomes institutionalized and politics prevails over it. This explains why political opposition in Iran originates both from the religious establishment and from non-Islamic groups, also from within the Iranian government as well as from without. For example, Ayatollahs Hossein Montazeri, Abdolkarim Moussavi Ardebili, Mohamed Hossein Kazemini Borujerdi, and Safi Golpaygani have all publicly criticized the military and secret police.

In 2009, Ayatollah Montazeri, who was instrumental in introducing the role of the guardian (as a political in addition to the moral authority) in 1979, went as far to proclaim Iranian leaders unfit to rule and called for their removal from positions of power. The reformist ayatollahs spoke publicly of how an Islamic system of governance must rest on the sovereignty of the people as well as the sovereignty of God. They have called for the redefinition of the position of supreme leader, demanding that he share power with a small council of other clerics, and for a consensus among *Shiite* clerics in the selection of a preeminent religious ruler. In their view, a reinterpretation of *wilayat al-faqih* could lead to a more representative leadership whereas the clergy would keep control over religious and social matters while giving up some political power. Whereas one clerical faction believes that a group of senior clerics should rule by consensus, another argues that leadership should be left to politicians who are devout but not necessarily clerics.[22]

From within the regime, in 2002, former President Khatami publicly questioned the authority of the clerical establishment to overturn legislative initiative. He called for changes in the constitution that would weaken their right to change the course of Iranian history to fit their version of a just society.[23] In 2011, President Ahmadinejad and his close political ally Mashaie, in an apparent attempt to weaken Iran's clergy, publicly questioned their monopoly of interpretation of the Islamic textual sources. Predictably, the attempt to take Iran in a new direction has prompted accusations from high-ranking clerics including Ayatollah Mesbah Yazdi, a longtime mentor of President Ahmadinejad, who interpreted the challenge to supreme clerical rule as an act against the foundation of the Islamic political system. Yazdi asserted the key role of scholars in interpreting Islam.[24]

Chapter 17

Islamism and Political Opposition

Opposition to clerical rule in a Muslim state, similar to the one voiced among some Iranian clerics, extends to other *Shia* religious groups in Iraq, Lebanon, and Bahrain. For example, the dominant *Shiite* theological school in Najaf (Iraq) rejects Khomeini's model and is critical of the notion of clerics seizing political power directly. Similarly, Bahrain's *Shia* elements (the al-Haqq Movement) reportedly also reject Islamic-based government.[1] A debate among the *Shia* religious groups currently centers on the issue of how much to distance religion from the governing structures of the state; in the *Sunni* Muslim community, the debate has most recently moved in the direction of how closely Islam should be brought into the state's institutions and administrative practices. In each case, of course, the debate is driven by historical events and the political opportunities associated with them.

Among the *Shia* clerics, the central point of reference is the 1979 Iranian revolution and the consequent appropriation of state powers by the religious establishment in Iran. The 2011 regime changes of Tunisia, Egypt, and Libya (all *Sunni*-majority states), and the subsequent commanding presence of Islamists in the politics of each, provided a historical opportunity for laymen *Sunni* Islamists and religious scholars alike to more aggressively assert their religious agenda. The certainty of constitutional changes created the opportunities for various Islamic groups to seek the greater role of Islam in the legal, judicial, economic, and educational systems of the state. It should be pointed out, however, that *Sunni* Muslims often differ, both cross-nationally and within individual national contexts, over the contents of their socially conservative political agenda and the extent of the involvement of the state institutions in Islamizing society. What they do agree on, and what ostensibly has a great appeal to a large number of voters across the Muslim world, is that the coming to power of the politically well-organized Islamists holds promise of an accountable government, free of corruption and repressive methods of governing. It is the promise of accountable government that drives large numbers of voters to the polls and explains their significant support for Islamist political parties in some *Sunni*-majority states such as Morocco, Tunisia, and Egypt.

Prior to the 2011 regime changes in the Middle East and North Africa, the accountability of the executive (royal or presidential) state power was very limited.[2] In most Arab countries, the chief executive could often be constitutionally empowered to dismiss parliament arbitrarily, legislate by executive decree, form governments by ignoring parliamentary results, appoint and dismiss members of the judiciary, and bypass the judiciary altogether through the creation of executive-controlled "security courts." The rule of law and basic human rights such as freedom of speech, assembly, and religion were either non-existent entirely (e.g., Saudi Arabia) or were in a rudimentary form (e.g., Egypt, Jordan, and Kuwait). Until January 2011, with no exceptions, in the twenty-two members of the Arab League, there was no rotation of political power, no substantive redistribution of power, and no creation of effective checks and balances at the institutional level to limit executive power. Occasional external pressures for democratization led to some competitive elections (e.g., Jordan in 1989 and Egypt in 2005) but the top-down democratization would be calibrated to avoid any substantive political changes. In each case, the surge of electoral support for Islamists (Jordan, Algeria, Egypt, and the Palestinian territories) provided a pretext for rulers to block any further movement.

Little or no influence over policy within their own states, combined with their inability to replace the unaccountable rulers and the fears that public expression of dissent would be brutally punished, left the Muslim public with the feeling of political impotence. As repeated crises made the state vulnerable, they eventually created political openings for Islamists. Although outlawed and persecuted, they operated through their own networks of mosques and underground organizations like the Libyan Islamic Fighting Group and the Muslim Brotherhood. The fact that Islamists were not tainted by a connection to corrupt regimes made them succeed in carving out substantial constituencies and present themselves as the primary, if not the only, opposition to the incumbent regimes. Islamism has a core group of ardent supporters but has also mobilized people who had been excluded from the political process. It also extends to numerous segments of the population who have in various ways and to different degrees turned to Islam. This is an antigovernment Islamism, driven primarily by domestic politics.

Chapter 18

Political Opposition in a Variety of National Contexts

For Islamists across the Muslim countries, their religion is a major component of the strategy to mobilize their respective constituencies. This is why they share principle objectives and employ similar rhetoric. In general, Islamist political parties make the adoption of *sharia* the most prominent issue in their political platforms and use Islamic ideals as a reference for criticizing what they perceive as authoritarian, corrupt, incompetent, and illegitimate regimes. They sometimes oppose the secular justification of political rule and the expansion of state power and capacity that stems from the state-sponsored secularization of society and regard Islam integral to politics and society. Their stated goals include the establishment of a state that would be governed through Islamic law and "Islamic values" (or "the spirit of Islam"). Yet, sharia is not universally applied in any Islamic country and the Islamic legal tradition is too diverse, diffuse, and amorphous to be implemented in a uniformed way. Principal political differences over issues such as what should be the relationship with both traditional ulama and orthodox *Sufi* orders also matter. As a result, there is a lot of variation among Islamists, within what to non-Muslims worldwide may appear as monolithic political movement or ideology.

In Islam, much like in Christianity, the relationship between state and religion has been mediated by local circumstances, by particular social and economic processes that operate locally.[1] Frequently, Islamists' actions are driven more by nationalist considerations than by religious ones and specific political conditions clearly affect their platforms and political activities. Factors such as political history and civil-military relations, among others, help explain much of the variation in Islamists' policies across the Muslim world. For example, Tunisia's nearly two centuries of constitutional history influenced its *al-Nahdha* Islamist party (the party of Islamic Renewal) and incorporates both a French-style gender equality code and a liberal interpretation of *sharia* law into its platform. Whereas Islamists in Libya, the country which remarkably lacks similar constitutional tradition, the Transitional National Council (TNC) publicly promoted polygamy as a means of social control.[2] In some cases, such as Turkey or Indonesia, the active role of the military in the country's politics, until relatively recently, severely limited the political space that resident Islamist groups could carve up for themselves and arguably lastingly neutralized the effects of Islamism.

Similarly, political extremism of Islamist groups varies cross-nationally in at least two ways. First, it varies according to inclusion or exclusion from the political process. For example, if allowed to participate legally in the political process, Islamist groups generally become more moderate; when outlawed, they have a tendency to become radicalized. Thus, the legal involvement of the *Jamiaat-i-Islami* (Pakistan), the Party for Justice and Development (Morocco) and the Islamic Action Front (Jordan), in their respective national environments, apparently provided no negative incentives for them to adopt extremist agenda and tactics. But severe structural limitations of choice of the Tunisian Islamic Movement in Tunisia or the earlier described brutal repression of the Egyptian state applied against the Muslim Brotherhood, made those two groups radical in the past. Second, geographic proximity of the Islamists to the armed confrontation pitting Muslims against non-Muslims also affect the choices of policies and tactics. The examples include Islamist groups such as Hamas in the Palestinian territories and Hezbollah in Lebanon, where the Palestinian issue is in large part responsible for political radicalization, and the Pakistani-based group *Lashkar-e-Tayiba* that has been active in a highly disputed Kashmir region.

Second, economic conditions in the national environments in which Islamists operate, such as the availability of economic opportunities and the level of integration into the international economy, also play a role in shaping political programs of Islamists. For example, the moderation of Islamism in Turkey, Indonesia, and Malaysia compared to other majority-Muslim countries could in part be explained by the export-oriented nature of their economies and their consequent greater integration into the international economy.

Chapter 19

Endorsement of Parliamentary Politics: A Tactic or a Substantive Shift?

A number of Islamist movements began as single-issue parties, challenging existing laws and instituting *sharia* law. Beginning in the 1990s, however, they noticeably shifted their focus on democratic reform, publicly committing themselves to the alternation of power, popular sovereignty, and judicial independence. Mainstream Islamists, such as the Muslim Brotherhood, have seemingly abandoned the project of an Islamic state and instead emphasize other themes, such as the demand for justice (*al-adala*) and freedom (*al-hurriya*). The Brotherhood accepted democracy as being compatible with its notion of slow Islamization. It justified democracy on Islamic grounds claiming that "the *umma* [the Muslim community] is the source of *sulta* [political authority]" and reformulated "traditional Islamist thinking to incorporate concepts of human rights, pluralism, and democracy."[1]

The Brotherhood thus viewed free elections as the only legitimate method for selecting a leader where leaders are required to consult with the people or their representatives via a process of *shura*, or consultation. This is consistent with Islamic constitutionalists who argue that a parliament is the most effective institution for enabling the public to participate in the drafting of laws in the areas not covered under Islamic law.[2] The Brotherhood members have formed electoral alliances with secular political forces in the country, most notably with the labor unions, nationalists, and liberals. The Brotherhood's 2004 Reform Initiative emphasized support for "a republican, parliamentary, constitutional and democratic political order in the framework of the principles of Islam."[3] Since 2005, the Muslim Brotherhood parliamentary bloc has emerged as one of the most vocal critics of the authoritarian regime. Following the 2011 regime change, the group was legalized, and in April 2011 it launched a civic political party called the Freedom and Justice Party (Egypt) to contest elections. So does the Jordanian branch of the Muslim Brotherhood, a legal group that uses peaceful methods and participates in election through its political wing, the Islamic Action Front.[4]

The Brotherhood's endorsement of parliamentary politics is part of a broader trend among Islamist organizations and movements across the Muslim world. Staying within the Arab countries, the Islamist Justice and Development Party in Morocco used to insist on the inclusion of Islamic law into the legal system of the state and called for a revolutionary change. Now it accepts the legitimacy of the Moroccan monarchy and limits its political activism to what it describes as "the protection of Islamic identities."[5] It sees Morocco as already an Islamic state, which makes Islamization unnecessary.[6] In 2005, the party adopted a new, more liberal version of the *mudawwana* (the code regulating marriage and family life in the country) that seemingly improves women's social status in Moroccan society.[7] The above mentioned Jordanian Islamic Action Front claims to be committed to democracy, human rights, and a gradual political reform. About 10 percent of its membership are women and the organization actively recruits female members and educates women on their rights.[8] Hadas, Kuwait's Islamic constitutional movement (the branch of the Muslim Brotherhood) created in 1991 calls for political party pluralism and has developed a political agenda offering support for new mothers, divorcees, and women married to non-Kuwaitis.[9] Finally the Islah ("Reform") movement in Somalia is committed to democratic values and tolerance of different religions and races; it engages in peaceful programs to promote social justice.

Outside the Arab world, the two instructive examples are that of Malaysia and Tajikistan. Despite its radical Islamist political agenda in the 1950s and again in the 1980s, the Malaysian Pan-Malysian Islamic Party (PAS) now appears committed to electoral politics and democratic institutions.[10] The party has also demonstrated tolerance towards non-Islamic parties. Similarly, the Tajikistan's Islamic Renaissance Party, which at one point had been involved in a bloody civil war with a secular authoritarian state has seemingly abandoned its revolutionary Islamist agenda and has accepted elections and parliamentary politics. It has since turned to a promotion of women's role in society, specifically in the political arena and is cultivating the image of a party that has moved away from its more conservative religious base in the rural areas and more towards educated classes in the urban areas.

But how sincere is this shift to democratic politics? Was it just a pragmatic move to take advantage of a limited opportunity to get involved in parliamentary politics? In their public statements, the Muslim Brotherhood members, both in Egypt and in the organization's branches abroad, deliberately maintain ambiguities on a range of highly contentious issues such as the scope of political pluralism, restrictions to personal and civil liberties, the status of women, the place of religious minorities, the toleration of secular Muslims, or acceptable uses of violence. The Muslim Brotherhood's rejection of violence at home does not extend to areas where Muslims live under occupation, such as the Palestinian territories or Iraq. In 2007, it distributed a draft program for its proposed political party, which called for a ban on women or minority Coptic Christians from competing for the Egyptian presidency. In this view, only Muslims would be eligible for the Egyptian presidency on the grounds that the president has powers of oversight on Islamic issues.

The reasons for the ambiguity of specifically Egyptian Brotherhood members are manifold. In part, they result from a generational gap between the group's authoritarian and conservative leadership, on the one hand, and its younger (reformist) members, on the other. The latter have been pushing for more transparency within the organization, more sustained political engagement, increased cooperation with other movements across ideological lines, and a less austere approach to cultural issues.[11] But the ambiguities of Muslim Brotherhood members also result from the decades of ideological adaptation in response to repressive policies of the Egyptian government. If so, the apparent shift in support of democratic structures and human rights could indeed be tactical rather than substantive. Finally, the organization's character and goals also have a tendency to vary from community to community, making it difficult to discern the organization's policies.

Both the Islamic Action Front in Jordan and the Party of Justice and Development (PJD) in Morocco reject violence and terrorism, and claim to be loyal to their respective monarchies.[12] At the same time, both parties operate in the face of significant political barriers. In the 2002 elections, the PJD only fielded candidates in 55 of 91 districts, as it feared winning the election and triggering a repressive response from the Moroccan government similar to what happened in Algeria when an Islamist party became too popular.[13] The IAF in Jordan claims to oppose only certain government policies and not the Jordanian monarchical regime, although it competes in the electoral system that prevents it from winning a majority in parliament.[14] Moreover, although it claims not to seek revolutionary change, it harbors a vocal faction of radicals.[15] Lastly, the decision of the leadership of the Egypt-based al-Jama'a, serving time in jail, to give up violence in 1997 was endorsed by most of its leaders operating outside of jail in March 1999. However, some extremist leaders and groups, especially the factions of the Egyptian Islamic *Jihad* denounced what they saw as the "capitulation" of the internal leadership.

Chapter 20

The Agents of Islamization in Majority-Muslim States: Religious Scholars or Islamists?

In both Saudi Arabia and Iran, the only two countries that claim to be ruled by Islamic law, the relationship between the state and religious establishment, as a whole, is not always cordial and, at times, could even be unstable. In the Saudi case, the monarchy, when faced with challenges to its specific policies by the scholars, sometimes extends concessions to them to reduce possible tensions. In that sense, the Saudi monarch occasionally faces some informal checks on his power from outside his innermost circles. At the same time, the Saudi monarch does not hesitate to purge the state institutions of the most conservative elements of the religious establishment that might pose a threat to the political regime. In Iran, the dictatorial power of the Supreme Leader may arguably be even greater than that of the Saudi monarch, as he, endowed with a self-proclaimed divine mandate, faces no comparable checks on his power. Although allegedly fused, the state power and religious authority in Iran do not overlap entirely, since political opposition to the state in Iran originates, in part, from the religious establishment. Moreover, not even the authority of the state power in Iran is coherent, as demonstrated by the repeated tensions between the Supreme Leader and the presidency of the state.

The political significance of religious scholars in both Saudi Arabia and Iran is a product of the evolution of the two states, and is in no way a pattern of development necessary to other majority-Muslim states. In most of the *Sunni*-majority

Muslim states, there has been an unwritten compact between the regime and the religious establishment by which the scholars have been allowed free rein in cultural and religious matters in return for their acquiescence to the state's control of the political and economic spheres. This political quietism of the *ulama* in the *Sunni* Muslim world can be traced back to al-Ghazali's proscription of quietism discussed in the earlier sections. There has been a significant cross-regional variation, however, in terms of the level of *ulama* involvement in public affairs. The scholars have traditionally played a more activist role in Southeast and South Asia. For example, the *ulama* have been in leadership positions in the Pan-Malayisan Islamic Party, one of the major political organizations in Malaysia since the 1950s. Indonesia's Islamic organizations—*Nahdlatul Ulama* and *Muhammadiyah*—both comprised of Muslim scholars, joined the Indonesia *Ulama* Council (MUI) in 2005 to work with the regime as a new task force against Islamist extremists. In Pakistan, the *ulama* based party, *Jamiat-ul-Ulama-i-Islam* has had some electoral success since the 1990s. However, until 2011, all three countries, Malaysia, Indonesia, and Pakistan, had more success in reconciling Islam with elections and parliamentary politics than any of the Arab states.

In the post-Mubarak or post-Ben Ali regimes of Egypt and Tunisia respectively, the salience of the *ulama* in public may increase. In Egypt, the al-Azhar University *fatwa* committee has signaled its intent to play a more activist role in public. As its own contribution to the public debates about constitutional choices in the post-Mubarak state, al-Azhar published, in 2011, an eleven-point document that proposed freedom of opinion, faith, and human rights in a state that would be "civilian, protected by constitution and law."[1] The Al-Azhar *ulama*, in an apparent attempt to reclaim its leadership role in the *Sunni* Muslim world, also mediated between liberal politicians and Islamists in their disputes over constitutional principles. The increased activism of scholars in Egypt or Tunisia does not necessarily threaten to undermine the efforts to create representative and accountable governments in those two countries. Among the Arab *Sunni* Muslims the greater threat may come from the laymen Islamists rather than from the *ulama* since the former and not the latter have held the holistic view of religion and state and have traditionally sought political power to impose a top-down Islamization of society. Neither Saudi

Arabia nor *Shia* Iran, however, will likely be their models, because both regimes have remarkably failed to create harmonious relationships between Islam and the state as well as accountable institutions. Even more significantly, in both Saudi Arabia and Iran, in contrast with Egypt or Tunisia, religious credentials are largely monopolized by scholars rather than by laymen Islamists.

Chapter 21

Islamists Subjected to Performance Tests

In the Arab *Sunni* world, the laymen Islamists are, in fact, involved in a two-way competition. On the one hand, they compete for the recognition of their religious credentials; on the other, they contest for political power like any other political organization. With the lifting of restrictions on the involvement of religious organizations in politics that resulted from the 2011 regime changes in the Middle East and North Africa, Islamists are in competition for religious credentials in a highly competitive struggle for religious authority that has been significantly decentralized in *Sunni* Islam since the end of the caliphate in 1924. By accepting the rules of electoral politics, the Islamists make themselves subject to transparency and performance tests. Once in office, Islamists are objects of scrutiny as are other political groups. The Turkish Justice and Development Party, arguably Islamist—a description the Party itself rejects—has governed the country since 2002 with significant success as manifested in two successive re-elections (in 2007 and 2011). The Muslim Brotherhood has also had success in promoting social and public health policies in the Egyptian parliament since the late 1990s.

However, the governance of Islamic parties elsewhere has been less successful due to their incompetence or to charges of corruption. In the 1990s in Yemen, for example, an Islamic party, Islah, became part of a coalition government and took the portfolio of the Education Ministry. After showing incompetence at governing, Islamists lost their support in the following election.[1] In Indonesia, Abdurrahman Wahid, a democratically elected president in 1998 and a leader of the largest

Islamic movement, the *Nadlatul Ulama*, was impeached by the Indonesia national parliament in 2001 over allegations of corruption in his administration.

The example of Indonesia is instructive also because of the 2004 parliamentary elections there. The Islamist Prosperous Justice Party (PKS) played up its anticorruption platform (the party otherwise considered to be the most Islamist and *sharia*-oriented in its approach). The secular-inclusive Muslim parties won close to a third of the votes. Once the Islamic parties were in office, their pristine image was tarnished. Several of the PKS lawmakers were prosecuted in corruption cases. Moreover, the Islamist parties angered many Indonesians by pressing hard on several symbolic religious issues (a vague "anti-pornography" and a ban on an "erotic" dance called *jaipong* that many regard as part of their cultural heritage). As a result, in the next election in 2009, voters punished Islamic parties (the PKS and others) that narrowly focused on religious issues (suffering a drop in support from more than a third to slightly over a quarter of the vote). Even the PKS's best efforts to appeal to the country's mainstream (the Prosperous Justice Party, ran television commercials of young women without headscarves and distributed pamphlets in the colors of the country's major secular parties) failed to sway the public.[2]

Conclusion

Staying on message from God in the early Muslim community assumed a virtual overlap of religious, moral, and political authority under the mantle of Prophet Muhammad. The growth of the Muslim community, on the one hand, and the issue of succession of the Prophet's mantle, on the other, generated a plurality of views of how to maintain a unity of authority in line with Islamic teachings. The successive models of political order in the Muslim community—the dynastic state, the empire, and the nation-state—each has been unable to restore the holistic ideal of religious, moral, and political that is believed by Muslims to have prevailed in the city-state of Medina. With the dispersal and discontinuity of religious and political authority, the *sharia*, particularly in *Sunni* Islam, developed as a key in maintaining a belief in the Muslim community of staying on message from God. As the *sharia*, starting with the mid-nineteenth century, became progressively marginalized and was replaced with secular legal codes, the Muslim community lost not only a normative religious order but also a key source of political authority. The repeated failures of the secular authority, in the form of constitutional monarchies and republics, eventually invited the movements calling for the restoration of a normative order based on the *sharia* and sought political authority in order to do so.

This book traces the process described above and focuses specifically on three critical historical junctures: first, the early expansion of the Muslim community from the city-state of Medina to the Umayyad and Abassyd empires between the seventh and tenth centuries AD; second, the creation of nation states in the last two decades of the nineteenth century and the third decade of the twentieth century; and third, the quest for an accountable state that started with the Islamist movements back in the 1920s and 1930s, intensified in the 1970s, and culminated with the series of social uprisings against the incumbent regimes in early 2011.

Each of the three historical periods raised the issue of legitimacy of political governance and the constitutional place of Islam in a Muslim state. Each triggered revivalist movements that sought to restore religious purity believed to have defined the early Islamic community of Prophet Muhammad and the rightly guided caliphs. Of the three, however, only the last one initiated the movements—Islamists as they came to be called—that also aspired to taking political power and that were driven (in *Sunni* Islam) primarily by laymen rather than by religious scholars.

Islamism, as this book has shown, marks the continuation of the revivalist tradition in Islam and the tradition of cyclical challenges to the perceived deviation from the true path of God. In part, Islamism was a reaction to the fragmentation and secularization of the Muslims brought upon by foreign, Western influence, mostly in the second part of the nineteenth century. But also, it was a direct product of foreign-imported modernization of the time that put faith in a state as a principle source of socialization and agency of social change. The catch-all phrase "Islamism" stands for a variety of social and political movements that share the commitment to the restoration of political and economic justice but differ on the level of acceptance of political systems in which they operate, strategies they employ, and both immediate and long-term political objectives. Cross-national and cross-regional variation among the Islamist movements are a result of social, economic, and political conditions in the individual Muslim majority states in which they are based as well as from the nature and scope of external interferences of a number of influential actors including but not limited to Iran, Israel, Pakistan, Saudi Arabia, Turkey, and the United States.

This book acknowledges the existence of the violent offshoots of Islamist organizations and movements; it explains their origins and discusses some of the reasons for their continued presence. It also recognizes that there are Islamist fundamental movements for the restoration of the *sharia* that are driven by the desire of religious purity and seem to be willing to accept the lifestyle of the early practitioners of Islam in the seventh century AD. However, the book's focus is mostly on the Islamist movements and organizations that have a history of participating in electoral and parliamentary politics, have held political offices in the past, and that claim to maintain their activism in order to seek an accountable Muslim state. Having maintained political relevance and resilience in opposing the incumbent authoritarian regimes in Egypt, Pakistan, Turkey, Indonesia, and numerous other Muslim majority countries over the several decades, Islamist movements and organizations are often best positioned to compete for electoral votes and win a substantial number of seats in national parliaments given free and fair elections. Parliamentary elections in Tunisia and Egypt, following the 2011 regime changes in each of those two countries, clearly confirm this assumption.

A direct access to political power forces Islamists to make a transition from a virtually permanent political opposition to the actual governance that would require bringing clarity to the issue of the constitutional role of Islam in their respective countries. Islamism has traditionally lacked specificity about concrete state institutions because Islamic sources provide no clear guidance in this regard and have given rise to different conceptions of political authority ranging from neopatrimonialism to democracy. Two constitutional issues are particularly important. The first is the extent to which the *sharia* would play a role in the legal system; whether the laws of the state ought simply not to be against Islam or whether they ought to be Islamic in their nature. In either case, the implementation of laws inevitably raises the question of a treatment of minority (non-Muslim) religious groups, women, or atheists. The second is the issue of the extent to which the *sharia* would play a role in a system of governance. In some instances, Islamists have invested too much hope in a political solution to what are essentially non-political (moral) issues and problems. For example, Islamist parties acting in political opposition have a history of censoring important works of philosophy, art, and literature. In some cases, they also wanted to ban theater, cinema, and arts such as sculpture of the human form. In all of those instances the issue at stake is whether the state has moral authority to enforce such rules.

The transition from political opposition to governance that seems to be upon the Islamists, of course, does not take place in a political vacuum. So the answers to the questions raised above are likely to be provided in the contexts not only of the requirements of immediacy and expedience of a governing process but also of significant political pressures both domestically and from abroad, from secular and religious groups alike. Some of the pressures, either domestic or external, may help radicalize Islamist groups in power and push them in the direction of a theocratic and authoritarian form of government. Islamists, in power, driven by political pragmatism may help depoliticize religion. Although public life in some majority Muslim countries has become more religious, this may be transitory and change once the Islamist groups are installed in power. Finally, religious authorities, as any other authorities, could themselves be corrupted by proximity to political power and consequently be either voted or forced out of power.

ENDNOTES

INTRODUCTION

1 Khaled M. Abou El Fadl, *The Great Theft*, p. 40.
2 Roy R. Andersen et al., *Politics and Change in the Middle East*, p. 134.
3 Noah Feldman, *The Fall and Rise of the Islamic State*, p. 111.
4 John L. Esposito, *Islam*, pp. 13–14.
5 Khaled M. Abou El Fadl, *The Great Theft*, p. 40.
6 Roy R. Andersen et al., *Politics and Change in the Middle East*, p. 134.

CHAPTER 1

1 Bill and Springborg, *Politics in the Middle East*, p. 34.
2 John L. Esposito, *Islam*, pp. 13–14.
3 Roy R. Andersen et al., *Politics and Change in the Middle East*, p. 10.
4 Karen Armstrong, *A History of God*.
5 Montgomery W. Watt, *Islamic Political Thought*, p. 28.
6 Karen Armstrong, *A History of God*.
7 Jean Jacques Rousseau, *The Social Contract*, p. 179.
8 Charles E. Butterworth, "Political Islam."
9 Bill and Springborg. *Politics in the Middle East*, p. 35.
10 John L. Esposito, *Islam*, p. 15.
11 Karen Armstrong, *A History of God*.
12 Roy R. Andersen et al., *Politics and Change in the Middle East*, p. 132.

CHAPTER 2

1 Bill and Springborg. *Politics in the Middle East*, p. 33.
2 John L. Esposito, *Islam*, p. 31.
3 Roy R. Andersen et al., *Politics and Change in the Middle East*, p. 41.
4 William L. Cleveland, *A History of the Modern Middle East*, p. 15.

5 Roy R. Andersen et al., *Politics and Change in the Middle East*, p. 39.

6 *Ibid.*, p. 29.

7 William L. Cleveland, *A History of the Modern Middle East*, p. 16.

8 Roy R. Andersen et al., *Politics and Change in the Middle East*, p. 29.

9 *Ibid.*, p. 30.

10 *Ibid.*

11 Montgomery W. Watt, *Islamic Political Thought*, p. 29.

12 Roy R. Andersen et al., *Politics and Change in the Middle East*, p. 4.

13 William L. Cleveland, *A History of the Modern Middle East*, p. 15.

14 *Ibid.*, p. 17.

15 *Ibid.*

16 Montgomery W. Watt, *Islamic Political Thought*, p. 29.

17 William L. Cleveland, *A History of the Modern Middle East*, p. 15.

18 Roy R. Andersen et al., *Politics and Change in the Middle East*, p. 30.

19 William L. Cleveland, *A History of the Modern Middle East*, p. 17.

20 Douglas E. Streusand, *Islamic Gunpowder Empires*, p. 12.

21 Roy R. Andersen et al., *Politics and Change in the Middle East*, p. 42.

22 Clifford Geertz, *Islam Observed*.

23 William L. Cleveland, *A History of the Modern Middle East*, p. 24.

24 Roy R. Andersen et al., *Politics and Change in the Middle East*, p. 27.

25 William L. Cleveland, *A History of the Modern Middle East*, p. 13.

26 *Ibid.*, 14.

27 Noah Feldman, *The Fall and Rise of the Islamic State*, p. 50.

28 *Ibid.*, p. 23.

29 Mohammed Ayoob, *The Many Faces of Political Islam*.

30 William L. Cleveland, *A History of the Modern Middle East*, p. 28.

31 Toni Johnson, "Sharia and Militancy."

32 Noah Feldman, *The Fall and Rise of the Islamic State*, pp. 26–27.

33 *Ibid.* p. 25.

34 Douglas E. Streusand, *Islamic Gunpowder Empires*, p. 15.

35 Noah Feldman, *The Fall and Rise of the Islamic State*, p. 28.

36 *Ibid.*, p. 55.

37 *Ibid.*

38 Roy R. Andersen et al., *Politics and Change in the Middle East*, p. 36.

39 Noah Feldman, *The Fall and Rise of the Islamic State*, p. 38.

40 *Ibid.*

41 Bill and Springborg. *Politics in the Middle East*, p. 35.

42 Mohammed Ayoob, *The Many Faces of Political Islam*.

43 Douglas E. Streusand, *Islamic Gunpowder Empires*, p. 18.

44 *Ibid.* p. 19.

45 Roy R. Andersen et al., *Politics and Change in the Middle East*, p. 31.

46 *Ibid.* p. 36.

47 Douglas E. Streusand, *Islamic Gunpowder Empires*, p. 23.

48 Noah Feldman, *The Fall and Rise of the Islamic State*, p. 54.

49 H. Inalcik, *The Ottoman Empire*, p. 68.

50 William L. Cleveland, *A History of the Modern Middle East*, p. 42.

51 *Ibid.*, 29.

52 *Ibid.*

53 Roy R. Andersen et al., *Politics and Change in the Middle East*, p. 39.

CHAPTER 3

1 Bill and Springborg, *Politics in the Middle East*, p. 35.

2 John L. Esposito, *Unholy War*, p. 45.

3 William L. Cleveland, *A History of the Modern Middle*, pp. 122–123.

4 John L. Esposito, *Unholy War*, p. 47.

5 Roy R. Andersen et al., *Politics and Change in the Middle East*, p. 41.

6 Khaled M. Abou El Fadl, *The Great Theft*, p. 47.

7 William L. Cleveland, *A History of the Modern Middle*, pp. 122–123.

8 Khaled M. Abou El Fadl, *The Great Theft*, p. 52.

CHAPTER 4

1 Jürgen Habermas, *The Theory of Communicative Action*, p. 258.

2 *Ibid.*, 260.

CHAPTER 5

1 Richard Bulliet, "Lecture 11: Change and Popular Culture."

2 *Ibid.*

3 Khaled M. Abou El Fadl, *The Great Theft*, p. 35.

4 William L. Cleveland, *A History of the Modern Middle*, p. 84.

5 Seyyed Vali Reza Nasr, *Islamic Leviathan*.

6 William L. Cleveland, *A History of the Modern Middle*, p. 59.

7 Richard Bulliet, "Lecture 9: Secular Nationalism."

8 William L. Cleveland, *A History of the Modern Middle*, p. 69.

9 Sevinc Sevda Kilicalp, *Centralization of the Ottoman State*.

10 Noah Feldman, *The Fall and Rise of the Islamic State*, p. 52.

11 *Ibid.*, p. 84.

12 Roy R. Andersen et al., *Politics and Change in the Middle East*, p. 344.

13 William L. Cleveland, *A History of the Modern Middle*, p. 83.

14 Richard Bulliet, "Lecture 9: Secular Nationalism."

15 Bill and Springborg, *Politics in the Middle East*, p. 29.

CHAPTER 6

1 Richard Bulliet, "Lecture 9: Secular Nationalism."

2 William L. Cleveland, *A History of the Modern Middle*, p. 138.

3 *Ibid.*, p. 150.

4 *Ibid.*, p. 153.

5 Noah Feldman, *The Fall and Rise of the Islamic State*, p. 86–87.

6 Richard Bulliet, "Lecture 9: Secular Nationalism."

CHAPTER 7

1 William L. Cleveland, *A History of the Modern Middle*, p. 128.

2 Richard Bulliet, "Lecture 9: Secular Nationalism."

3 Shibley Telhami and Michael Barnett (Eds) *Identity and Foreign Policy*.

4 Karen Armstrong, *A History of God*, p. 366.

CHAPTER 8

1 Seyyed Vali Reza Nasr, *Islamic Leviathan*.

2 *Ibid.*

3 Noah Feldman, *The Fall and Rise of the Islamic State*, p. 82.

4 Richard Bulliet, "Lecture 9: Secular Nationalism."

5 Bill and Springborg, *Politics in the Middle East*, p. 31.

6 Noah Feldman, *The Fall and Rise of the Islamic State*, p. 86.

7 Phebe Marr, *The Modern History of Iraq*.

CHAPTER 9

1 Richard Bulliet, "Lecture 9: Secular Nationalism."

2 S. S. Hasan, *Christians versus Muslims in Modern Egypt*, p. 169.

3 Roy R. Andersen et al., *Politics and Change in the Middle East*, p. 110.

4   Khaled M. Abou El Fadl, *The Great Theft*, p. 42.

5   Seyyed Vali Reza Nasr, *Islamic Leviathan*.

6   *Ibid.*

CHAPTER 10

1   William L. Cleveland, *A History of the Modern Middle*, p. 109.

2   *Ibid.*, p. 52.

3   Richard Bulliet, "Lecture 12: Iran in the 19th Century."

4   *Ibid.*

5   Roy Mottahedeh, *The Mantle of the Prophet*.

6   William L. Cleveland, *A History of the Modern Middle*, p. 113.

7   *Ibid.*, p. 117.

8   *Ibid.*, p. 187.

9   *Ibid.*

CHAPTER 11

1   Charles E. Butterworth, "*Political Islam*," p. 34.

2   Roy Mottahedeh, *The Mantle of the Prophet*, pp. 184–185.

3   *Ibid.*

4   Charles E. Butterworth, "*Political Islam*," p. 34.

5   William L. Cleveland, *A History of the Modern Middle*, p. 120.

CHAPTER 12

1   Richard Bulliet, "Lecture 18: The Question of Islamic Authority."

2   Reinhard Shulze, *A Modern History of the Islamic World*.

CHAPTER 13

1   Richard Mitchell, *The Society of the Muslim Brothers*, p. 12.

2   Nicola Pratt, *Democracy and Authoritarianism in the Arab World*.

3   Tal, Nahman, *Radical Islam in Egypt and Jordan*, p. 49.

4   *Ibid.*

5   Roxanne L. Euben, "Comparative Political Theory."

6   Abdullahi Ahmed An-Na'im, *Islam and the Secular State*.

7   Mohammed Ayoob, *The Many Faces of Political Islam*.

CHAPTER 14

1   Roxanne L. Euben, "Comparative Political Theory."

2 *Ibid.*

3 Khaled M. Abou El Fadl, *The Great Theft*, pp. 81–82.

CHAPTER 15

1 John L. Esposito, *Unholy War*, p. 106.

2 Bill and Springborg, *Politics in the Middle East*, p. 25.

3 John L. Esposito, *Unholy War*, p. 108.

4 Thomas Hegghammer, *Jihad in Saudi Arabia*, p. 17.

5 John L. Esposito, *Unholy War*, p. 108.

6 Thomas Hegghammer, *Jihad in Saudi Arabia*, p. 16.

7 John L. Esposito, *Unholy War*, p. 49.

8 Thomas Hegghammer, *Jihad in Saudi Arabia*, p. 17.

9 Bruce Riedel, "Al Qaeda's Surprising New Target" and Mark Burges "In the Spotlight."

CHAPTER 16

1 Michael Willis, *The Islamist Challenge*, p. 23.

2 Thomas Hegghammer, *Islamist Violence*, p 705.

3 Seyyed Vali Reza Nasr, *Islamic Leviathan*, p. 16.

4 Thomas Hegghammer, *Islamist Violence*, p. 705.

5 John R. Bradley "Saudi Arabia's Invisible Hand."

6 Hamied Ansari. *Egypt, The Stalled Society.*

7 Albrecht Holger, "How Can Opposition Support Authoritarianism?"

8 P.J. Vatikiotis, *The Egyptian Army in Politics.*

9 Israel Elad-Altman, *Democracy, Elections and the Egyptian Muslim Brotherhood.*

10 Lisa Blaydes, *Elections and Distributive Politics.*

11 Kienle Eberhard, *A Grand Delusion.*

12 Lisa Blaydes, *Elections and Distributive Politics.*

13 *Ibid.*

14 Seyyed Vali Reza Nasr, *Islamic Leviathan*, p.16.

15 Dexter Flikins, *The Journalist and the Spies.*

16 Shaul Bakhash, *The Reign of the Ayatollahs.*

17 *Ibid.*

18 Mohammad Bazzi, "Khomeini's Long Shadow."

19 *Ibid.*

20 Akbar Ganji, "The Struggle Against Sultanism."

21 Abdullahi Ahmed An-Na'im, *Islam and the Secular State.*

22 Mohammad Bazzi, "Khomeini's Long Shadow."

23 Roy R. Andersen et al., *Politics and Change in the Middle East*, p. 121.

24 Geneive Abdo, "Rooting for Khamenei."

CHAPTER 17

1 Justin Gengler, How Radical are Bahrain's Shia?

2 Ottaway, Marina, and Riley, Meredith. "Morocco: From Top-Down Reform," p. 3.

CHAPTER 18

1 Clifford Geertz, *Islam Observed*.

2 Ahmed Charai and Joseph Braude, "The Islamist Bloc?"

CHAPTER 19

1 Nicola Pratt, *Democracy and Authoritarianism in the Arab World*.

2 Bruce Rutherford, "What do Egypt's Islamists Want?"

3 Israel Elad-Altman, Democracy, Elections and the Egyptian Muslim Brotherhood.

4 Barry Rubin, *The Muslim Brotherhood*, p. 11.

5 Amr Hamzawy "Party for Justice and Development," p. 10.

6 Samir Amghar, "Political *Islam* in Morocco," p. 3.

7 Amr Hamzawy, "Party for Justice and Development," p. 9.

8 Escobar Stemmann, Juan Jose, "Islamic Activism in Jordan," p. 6.

9 Nathan J. Brown, "Kuwait's 2008 Parliamentary Elections."

10 Joseph Chin Yong Liow, "Exigency or Expediency?" p. 368.

11 Gilles Kepel, "Bin Laden Was Dead Already."

12 Shadi Hamid, "Engaging Political Islam to Promote Democracy," p. 3.

13 Ottaway, Marina, and Riley, Meredith, "Morocco: From Top-Down Reform," p. 14.

14 Nathan J. Brown, "Jordan and Its Islamic Movement," p. 19.

15 *Ibid.*, p. 8.

CHAPTER 20

1 Yasmine Saleh, "Egypt Islamic body blossoms."

CHAPTER 21

1 Nicholas D. Kristof, "Free the Hatemongers!"

2 Norimitsu Onishi, "Indonesia's Voters Retreat from Radical *Islam*."

BILBLIOGRAPHY

Abdo, Geneive. "Rooting for Khamenei." *Foreign Policy*. 10 May 2011.
  http://mideast.foreignpolicy.com/posts/2011/05/10/Rooting_for_Khamenei
  (Accessed May 15, 2011).

Abou El Fadl, Khaled M. *The Great Theft*: Wrestling *Islam from the Extremists*. New York, NY:
  Harper One, 2007.

Albrecht, Holger. "How Can Opposition Support Authoritarianism? Lessons from Egypt."
  Democratization, 12, 3, (2005): 378–397.

Ali M. Ansari. *Confronting Iran: The Failure of American Foreign Policy and the Next Great
  Crisis in the Middle*. New York, NY: Perseus Books Group, 2006.

Amghar, Samir. "Political Islam in Morocco." *CEPS Working Document 269*. Brussels: Center
  for European Policy Studies (June 2007): 1–10.

Andersen, Roy R. and Robert Seibert and Jon Wagner. *Politics and Change in the Middle East:
  Sources of Conflict and Accommodation*. Upper Saddle River, New Jersey: Prentice Hall,
  2008 (Ninth edition).

An-Na`im, Abdullahi Ahmed. *Islam and the Secular State: Negotiating the Future of Shari`a*.
  Cambridge, MA: Harvard University Press, 2008.

Ansari, Hamied. *Egypt, the Stalled Society*. Albany, NY: State University of New York Press,
  1986.

Armstrong, Karen. *A History of God: The 4,000-Year Quest of Judaism, Christianity and Islam*.
  New York, New York: Ballantine Books, 1994.

Ayoob, Mohammed. *The Many Faces of Political Islam: Religion and Politics in the Muslim
  World*. Ann Arbor, Michigan: University of Michigan Press, 2007.

Bakhash, Shaul. *The Reign of the Ayatollahs: Iran and the Islamic Revolution*. New York, NY.
  Basic Books, 1984.

Bazzi, Mohamad. "Khomeini's Long Shadow: How a Quiet Revolution in Shiism Could Resolve
  the Crisis in Iran." *Foreign Affairs*, 21 Jun 2010,
  http://www.foreignaffairs.com/articles/66479/mohamad-bazzi/khomeinis-long-
  shadow?page=show (Accessed Sep 16, 2011).

Bill, James A. and Robert Springborg. *Politics in the Middle East*. Harlow, United Kingdom:
  Longman, 1999 (5th Edition).

Blaydes, Lisa A. *Elections and Distributive Politics in Mubarak's Egypt*. New York, NY: Cambridge University Press, 2010.

Bradley, John R. "Saudi Arabia's Invisible Hand in the Arab Spring, How the Kingdom is Wielding Influence across the Middle East." *Foreign Affairs*, Council on Foreign Relations. 13 Oct 2011. http://www.foreignaffairs.com/articles/136473/john-r-bradley/saudi-arabias-invisible-hand-in-the-arab-spring?page=show (Accessed Oct 15, 2011).

Brown, Nathan J. "Jordan and Its Islamic Movement: The Limits of Inclusion?" *Carnegie Paper* 74. Washington, DC: Carnegie Endowment for International Peace, (November 2006): 3–23.

Brown, Nathan J. "Kuwait's 2008 Parliamentary Elections: A Setback for Democratic Islamism?" Carnegie Endowment. http://www.carnegieendowment.org/files/brown_kuwait2.pdf (Accessed May 24, 2011).

Bulliet, Richard. "Lecture 9: Secular Nationalism." Columbia University. History of the Modern Middle East. Columbia University, New York, NY. 17 Feb. 2009. http://www.openculture.com/history_free_courses (Accessed October 24, 2011).

_____. "Lecture 11: Change and Popular Culture: the Late 19th Century." Columbia University. History of the Modern Middle East. Columbia University, New York, NY. 24 Feb. 2009. http://www.openculture.com/history_free_courses (Accessed October 24, 2011).

_____. "Lecture 12: Iran in the 19th Century." Columbia University. History of the Modern Middle East. Columbia University, New York, NY. 26 Feb. 2009. http://www.openculture.com/history_free_courses (Accessed October 25, 2011).

_____. "Lecture 18: The Question of Islamic Authority." Columbia University. History of the Modern Middle East. Columbia University, New York, NY. 26 Feb. 2009. http://www.openculture.com/history_free_courses (Accessed October 25, 2011).

Burgess, Mark. "In the Spotlight: Islamic Movement of Uzbekistan." Center For Defense Information. http://www.cdi.org/terrorism/imu.cfm (Accessed May 23, 2011).

Butterworth, Charles E. "Political Islam: The Origins." *Annals of the American Academy of Political and Social Science* 524, (November 1992): 26-37.

Charai, Ahmed and Joseph Braude. "The Islamist Bloc?" *Foreign Policy*, November 4, 2011. http://www.foreignpolicy.com/articles/2011/11/04/the_islamist_bloc (Accessed November 12, 2011).

Cleveland, William L. *A History of the Modern Middle East*. Boulder, Colorado: Westview Press, 2008.

Dalrymple, William. "The Muslims in the Middle, *New York Times*, August 16, 2010. www.nyt.com, (accessed September 22, 2011).

Elad-Altman, Israel. "Democracy, Elections and the Egyptian Muslim Brothehood." *Current Trends in Islamist Ideology*, Vol. 3, February 16, 2006. (Accessed September 19, 2011).

Escobar Stemmann, Juan Jose. "Islamic Activism in Jordan." *Athena Intelligence Journal* 3.3 (July–September 2008) 7–18.

Esposito, John L. *Unholy War: Terror in the Name of Islam*. New York, New York: Oxford University Press, 2003.

_____., Islam: The Straight Path. New York, New York: Oxford University Press, 2010.

Euben, Roxanne L. "Comparative Political Theory: An Islamic Fundamentalist Critique of Rationalism." *The Journal of Politics* 59, no. 1 (Feb. 1997): 28–55.

Fathi, Nazila. "What We Got Right." *Foreign Policy*, 7 June, 2010. http://www.foreignpolicy.com/articles/2010/06/07/what_we_got_right (Accessed June 15, 2010).

Feldman, Noah. *The Fall and Rise of the Islamic State*. Princeton, New Jersey: Princeton University Press, 2008.

Filkins, Dexter. "The Journalist and the Spies: The Murder of a Reporter Who Exposed Pakistan's Secrets." *The New Yorker*. 19 September 2011. http://www.newyorker.com/reporting/2011/09/19/110919fa_fact_filkins#ixzz1a8c30Wh (Accessed September 23, 2011).

Ganji, Akbar. "The Struggle against Sultanism." *The Journal of Democracy*, 16, no. 4 (October 2005): 38–51.

Geertz, Clifford. *Islam Observed*. Chicago, IL: The University of Chicago Press, 1968.

Gengler, Justin .The Real Source of Unrest in the Kingdom. *Foreign Affairs*, May 15, 2011, http://www.foreignaffairs.com/articles/67855/justin-gengler/how-radical-are-bahrains-shia (Accessed September 23, 2011).

Gerges, Fawaz A. *America and Political Islam: Clash of Cultures or Clash of Interests*. Cambridge University Press,1999.

Gerges, Fawaz A. *Journey of the Jihadist: Inside Muslim Militancy*. Harvest Books, 2007.

_____"The Latter-Day Sultan."*Foreign Affairs*, (November/December 2008) 45–66.

Habermas, Jürgen. *The Theory of Communicative Action, Volume 1: Reason and Rationalization of Society*. Boston, MA: Beacon Press, 1985.

_____. "Religion in the Public Sphere." *European Journal of Philosophy*, 14 (1) (April 2006): 1–25.

Hamid, Shadi. "Engaging Political Islam to Promote Democracy." *Policy Report*. Washington, DC: Progressive Policy Institute (June 2007): 1–10.

Hamzawy, Amr. "Party for Justice and Development in Morocco: Participation and its Discontents." *Middle East Program* 93 (2008): 1–27. http://www.carnegieendowment.org/files/cp93_hamzawy_pjd_final1.pdf.

Haqqani, Husain. 2005. "The Role of Islam in Pakistan's Future." *Washington Quarterly* 28 (1)(2005): 85–96. (Accessed September 5, 2010).

Hasan, S. S. *Christians versus Muslims in Modern Egypt: The Century-Long Struggle for Coptic Equality*. New York, NY: Oxford University Press, 2003.

Hegghammer, Thomas. "Islamist Violence and Regime Stability in Saudi Arabia." *International Affairs* 84, no. 4 (2008): 701–715.

_____. *Jihad in Saudi Arabia: Violence and Pan-Islamism since 1979* (Cambridge Middle East Studies). New York, NY: Cambridge University Press, 2010.

Howard, Philip N. *The Digital Origins of Dictatorship and Democracy: Information Technology and Political Islam.* Cambridge, MA: Oxford University Press, 2011.

Inalcik, H. *The Ottoman Empire: The Classical Age 1300–1600.* New York, NY: Aristide D. Caratzas, 1973.

Johnson, Toni. "Sharia and Militancy." *Council on Foreign Relations,* 30 Nov 2010. http://www.cfr.org/religion-and-politics/sharia-militancy/p19155 (Accessed Jul 3, 2011).

Kepel, Gilles. *Muslim Extremism in Egypt: The Prophet and Pharaoh.* Berkely, CA: University of California Press, 2003.

_____. "Bin Laden Was Dead Already." 7 May, 2011. *The New York Times,* www.nyt.com, (Accessed May 7, 2011).

Kienle, Eberhard. *A Grand Delusion: Democracy and Economic Reform in Egypt.* London: IB Tauris, 2000.

Kilicalp, Sevinc Sevda. *Centralization of the Ottoman State and Modernization of the Waqf System.* Bologna, Italy: Master in International Studies in Philanthropy, University of Bologna, July 2009, Fourth Edition.

Kinzer, Stephen. *All the Shah's Men: An American Coup and the Roots of Middle East Terror.* Hoboken, NJ: Wiley, 2008 (2nd edition).

Kristof, Nicholas D., "Free the Hatemongers!" 22 March, 2002. *The New York Times,* www.nyt.com. (Accessed March 22, 2009).

Leiken, Robert and Steven Brooke. "The Moderate Muslim Brotherhood." *Foreign Affairs,* 86. No. 2 (March/April 2007): 107–121.

Liow, Joseph Chin Yong, (2004). "Exigency or Expediency? Contextualizing Political Islam and the PAS Challenge in Malaysian Politics." *Third World Quarterly* 25(2): 359–372.

Majd, Hooman. *The Ayatollah Begs to Differ.* New York, NY: Doubleday (2008).

Marr, Phebe. *The Modern History of Iraq.* Boulder, CO: Westview Press, 2004 (Second Edition).

Mitchell, Richard. *The Society of the Muslim Brothers.* London, U.K.: Oxford University Press, 1969.

Molavi, Afshin. *The Soul of Iran: A Nation's Journey to Freedom.* New York, NY: W. W. Norton; 2005 (Revised Edition).

Moore, Clement Henry. *Tunisia since Independence: the Dynamics of One-Party Government.* Berkeley CA: University of California Press, 1965.

Mottahedeh, Roy. *The Mantle of the Prophet: Religion and Politics in Iran.* New York, NY: Simon & Schuster,1985.

Nasr, Seyyed Vali Reza. *Islamic Leviathan: Islam and the Making of State Power.* New York, NY: Oxford University Press, 2001.

Nasr, Vali. *The Shia Revival: How Conflicts within Islam Will Shape the Future.* New York, NY: W. W. Norton, 2007.

Norton, Augustus Richard. "Thwarted Politics: The Case of Egypt's Hizb Al-Wasat." In *Remaking Muslim Politics: Pluralism, Contestaiton, Democratizaiton*, Ed. Robert W. Hefner, 133–160. Princeton NJ: Princeton University Press, 2005.

O'Hanlon, Michael E. Pakistan's War of Choice, March 24, 2010, *The New York Times*, www.nyt.com, (accessed April 25, 2010).

Onishi, Norimitsu. "Indonesia's Voters Retreat from Radical Islam." 25 April, 2009. *The New York Times*, www.nyt.com, (accessed April 25, 2009).

_____, "Extremism Spreads Across Indonesian Penal Code." 28 October, 2009. *The New York Times*, www.nyt.com, (accessed October 28, 2009).

Ottaway, Marina, and Riley, Meredith. "Morocco: From Top-Down Reform to Democratic Transition?" *Carnegie Paper* 71. Washington, DC: Carnegie Endowment for International Peace, September 2006, 1–20.

Pratt, Nicola C. *Democracy and Authoritarianism in the Arab World*. Boulder, CO: Lynne Rienner, 2007.

Rabasa, Angel, Cheryl Benard, Lowell H. Schwartz, and Peter Sickle. "Building Moderate Muslim Networks, Center for Middle East Public Policy." The RAND Corporation. 2007.http://www.rand.org/pubs/monographs/2007/RAND_MG574.pdf (Accessed August, 16, 2010).

Ramadan, Tariq. *Western Muslims and the Future of Islam*. New York, NY: Oxford University. Press, 2004.

Riedel, Bruce. "Al Qaeda's Surprising New Target." *The Daily Beast*, http://www.brookings.edu/opinions/2010/0802_alqaeda_turkey_riedel.aspx. (Accessed August 16, 2010).

Rosefsky Wickham. "Carrie The Path to Moderation: Strategy and Learning in the Formation of Egypt's Wasat Party." *Comparative Politics* 36, no. 2 (2004): 206.

Rousseau, Jean Jacques. *The Social Contract*. Translated by M. Cranston. London, U.K.: Penguin Books, 1968.

Rubin, Barry Ed. *The Muslim Brotherhood: The Organization and Policies of a Global Islamist Movement*. New, York, NY: Palgrave Macmillan, 2010.

Rutherford, Bruce. "What do Egypt's Islamists Want? Moderate Islam and the Rise of Islamic Constitutionalism." *Middle East Journal*, 60(4), 2006.

Sachedina, Abdulaziz. *The Islamic Roots of Democratic Pluralism*. New York, NY: Oxford University Press, 2001.

Saleh, Yasmine. "Egypt Islamic body blossoms in Arab Spring, aims to regain independence," 9 September 2011, al Arabia News, http://english.alarabiya.net/ (accessed September 9, 2011).

Schmidt, John R. "The Unravelling of Pakistan." *Survival* 51 (3) (2009): 29–54.

Singh, Michael. "Iranian Re-Revolution: How the Green Movement Is Repeating Iranian History." *Foreign Affairs*, 26 July, 2010 http://www.foreignaffairs.com/articles/66499/michael-singh/iranian-re-revolution?page=2 (Accessed July 28, 2010).

Shulze, Reinhard. *A Modern History of the Islamic World*. New York, NY: NYU Press, 2002.

Streusand, Douglas E. *Islamic Gunpowder Empires: Ottomans, Safavids, and Mughals*. Boulder, Colorado: Westview Press, 2011.

Tal, Nahman. *Radical Islam in Egypt and Jordan*. Eastbourne, East Sussex, UK: Sussex Academic Press, 2005.

Telhami, Shibley. *The Stakes: America in the Middle East: The Consequences of Power and The Choice for Peace*. Boulder CO: Westview Press, 2003 (Reprint Edition).

_____ and Michael Barnett (Eds). *Identity and Foreign Policy in the Middle East*. Ithaca, NY: Cornell University Press, 2002.

Traub, James. "Islamic Democrats? *The New York Times*, 29 April 2007 www.nyt.com. (Accessed October 28, 2009).

Vatikiotis, P.J. *The Egyptian Army in Politics: Pattern for New Nations?* Bloomington: Indiana University Press, 1961.

Watt, W. Montgomery. *Islamic Political Thought: The Basic Concepts*. Edinburgh, Scotland, U.K.: Edinburgh University Press 1997.

Willis, Michael. *The Islamist Challenge in Algeria*. New York: New York UP, 1997.